FREE DVD      **FREE DVD**

Property & Casualty Exam DVD from Trivium Test Prep!

Dear Customer,

Thank you for purchasing from Trivium Test Prep! We're honored to help you prepare for your exam.

To show our appreciation, we're offering a **FREE *Property & Casualty Exam Essential Test Tips* DVD by Trivium Test Prep**. Our DVD includes 35 test preparation strategies that will make you successful on your big exam. All we ask is that you email us your feedback and describe your experience with our product. Amazing, awful, or just so-so: we want to hear what you have to say!

To receive your **FREE *Property & Casualty Exam Essential Test Tips* DVD**, please email us at 5star@triviumtestprep.com. Include "Free 5 Star" in the subject line and the following information in your email:

1. The title of the product you purchased.

2. Your rating from 1 – 5 (with 5 being the best).

3. Your feedback about the product, including how our materials helped you meet your goals and ways in which we can improve our products.

4. Your full name and shipping address so we can send your **FREE *Property & Casualty Exam Essential Test Tips* DVD**.

If you have any questions or concerns please feel free to contact us directly at 5star@triviumtestprep.com. Thank you!

- **Trivium Test Prep Team**

Table of Contents

INTRODUCTION

The modern practice of insurance is often traced back to the founding of The Fire House in London in May 1680 by Dr. Nicholas Barbon, after the Great Fire of London. From its creation, insurance has provided consumers with a way to deal with a reduction in value that arises from loss. In its 330-plus years of existence, the practice of insurance has provided more than $400 billion in annual policy benefits paid by more than 2,700 property and casualty insurers based in the United States alone (according to information provided by the American Insurance Association, an industry trade organization).

Purpose of this Review Course

This review manual is designed for those who are interested in passing their state licensing examination for property and/or casualty insurance. The information provided in this manual is based on the topics and concepts commonly found on the licensing exam administered in every state.

You should use this review course as a supplement to your state's approved pre-licensing course.

State-Specific Requirements

Each state has its own requirements for attempting the property and casualty insurance examination. A table of these requirements, including fees and pre-licensing course requirements, is provided in the appendix to this review manual.

Preparing for Your Licensing Exam

The licensing exam for a property and casualty insurance agent (and broker) typically consists of up to 150 multiple-choice questions (MCQs). You will be asked to select the best answer among a choice of possible responses. MCQs are written in a variety of ways; knowing the different types of questions and the forms in which they are written may help you quickly deduce the correct response to the question.

The types of questions commonly found on MCQ exams include: (1) scenario type; (2) all EXCEPT; (3) Roman numbers; and, (4) elimination.

Scenario Type Questions

On the following page is an example of a scenario type question:

> The Equipment Breakdown Protection coverage form is used to cover loss resulting from the breakdown of covered equipment. The resulting equipment breakdown simultaneously caused the breakdown of 2 additional covered pieces of equipment under the coverage. What is the number of breakdowns that occurred based on the Equipment Breakdown Protection coverage form?
>
> A. 4 breakdowns
>
> B. 3 breakdowns
>
> C. 2 breakdowns
>
> D. 1 breakdowns
>
> The correct answer is **D**.

In a scenario type of question, you are provided with a lot of information before the question is asked. With these types of questions, find the question being asked (*What is the number of breakdowns that occurred based on the Equipment Breakdown Protection coverage form?*) and work back in the question for the additional information you need to answer the question.

All EXCEPT Questions

A question, usually containing the word "except" (i.e. all of the following, EXCEPT), that will present a series of statements in which three of the responses will be true and one of the responses will be false. The false statement will be the answer to the question.

On the following page, you will find an example of an All EXCEPT type question:

> All of the following coverages are available in a commercial package policy EXCEPT:
>
> A. Commercial Auto Insurance
>
> B. Inland Marine Insurance
>
> C. Ocean Marine Insurance
>
> D. Equipment Breakdown Insurance

In this example, you would select choice C, the reason being that it is opposite choice B. By elimination, A and D would be part of a commercial package policy (which they are), leaving you to select between B and C as being the false choice. At the very least, with these types of questions you should be able to narrow your probability of success from 1 in 4 to 1 in 2 (much better odds for success.

Roman Numbers Questions

A question that uses Roman numerals creates a multi-level selection approach to deriving the correct response. An example of a question that uses Roman numerals is:

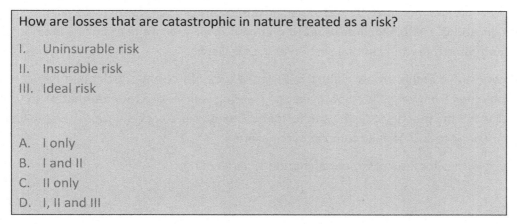

The correct answer is *C.* The key to answering a question with Roman numerals is by first selecting the incorrect response(s) to the question among the choices in Roman numerals (*i.e. I., II., III., IV., etc.*). In the example above, Choices I and III are incorrect responses. Looking at the answer choices at the alphabetic level (A, B, C, D) you can see that choice C is clearly the correct answer.

Elimination Questions

An elimination question is a type where the answer is easy to detect as a part of a process of elimination. After reading the question, the choice is made by eliminating the correct answers (or, conversely, eliminate the incorrect response).

> Which of the following is not a color?
>
> A. Blue
> B. Green
> C. Yellow
> D. Elephant

Basic Terms and Concepts

This review manual will present those terms and concepts that you will more than likely encounter on the licensing exam in **bold**. A complete definition of these terms and concepts features in the review material will also appear in the Key Definitions section, which is at the end of each chapter of this study guide.

Studying for the Licensing Examination

Your state's Property and Casualty Insurance licensing examination is going to test your knowledge in several areas dealing with types of coverage, forms, basic and general insurance concepts, and law. It is important to approach your review and preparation with a plan. Pace yourself so that you don't burn out or feel overwhelmed by the presented material.

Spending one to two hours a day over the course of up to two weeks should be sufficient time to review the material as well as master the content, as well as gain the confidence necessary to pass the exam on the first attempt.

Take the practice exams and measure your results against the correct answers and rationales provided for the questions. If you encounter a question that is in an area of the exam you are not familiar with, spend some more time in that section of your review.

The information presented in this review manual is designed to reinforce and supplement the knowledge you obtained from your state approved pre-licensing course. Use this information to confirm knowledge and the practice questions to further validate your comprehension and give you the confidence you need to successfully complete your exam.

Good luck and best wishes for a successful examination experience!

GENERAL INSURANCE CONCEPTS

There are basic concepts that are universal to all types of insurance. This holds true for property, casualty, fire, flood, liability, life and health insurance. An understanding of these concepts is important as they form the basis for the discussions on different types of insurance and their coverages.

RISK

Any type of insurance deals with insuring **risk** – the chance that a loss will occur. There are two types of risks, **speculative** risks and **pure** risks.

> - *Speculative risk* entails a chance for loss and gain. A good example of speculative risk is purchasing a lottery ticket.
> - *Pure risk* is the chance for loss with no possibility of gain. Injuries resulting from automobile accidents are an example of pure risk.

Peril

Risks evolve from a situation that increases the potential or serves as the cause of loss. This is known as a **peril**. Known perils include lightning, fire, wind, storms, water and ice.

Hazard

A **hazard** accelerates a *peril*; it is a condition or act that is a multiplier on the chance that the loss will occur. There are three types of hazards:

> - **Physical** hazard – a condition in the environment that increases the chance for loss (i.e. a banana peel left on the floor).
> - **Moral** hazard – engaging in an act of fraud or dishonesty (i.e. lying on an application for insurance in order to collect the benefit).
> - **Morale** hazard – indifference to a standard of conduct or law (i.e. drunk driving, speeding).

Elements of Insurable Risk

When an insurer looks at pure risk to insure, there are elements considered in order to determine whether such risk is acceptable and insurable or not. The elements of an *ideal* insurable risk includes:

1. The chance for loss (risk) must be spread among a large group of unrelated or unlike units.
2. The risk must be certain.
3. The nature of the risk should be accidental, unintentional and unexpected.
4. The result of the loss should create a financial hardship or reduction in value.
5. The loss must be calculable and the cost of insuring the risk affordable.
6. The loss may not include those perils that are catastrophic, such as major floods or terrorist attacks.

Adverse Selection

An insurance look at the elements of ideal risk in order to guard against adverse selection. **Adverse selection** is the opportunity of those whose risk is uninsurable to obtain insurance, to the detriment of those who are insurable. Those individuals belonging to an adverse risk group experience loss at a rate that is higher than individuals with average risk experience (see Figure 1.)

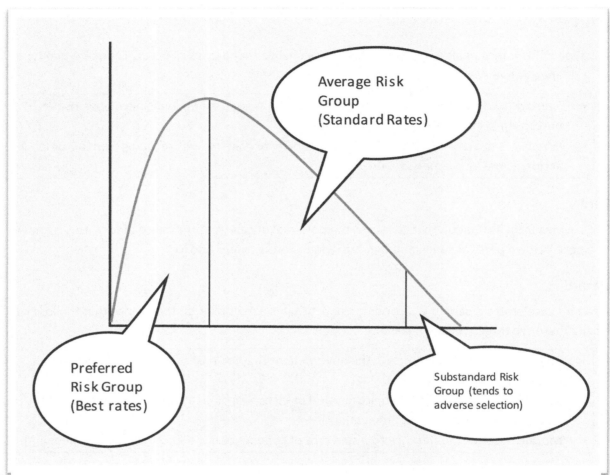

Figure 1: Distribution of insurable/uninsurable risk

Risk Management Techniques

There are methods used by insurance companies and the individuals insured to manage risk in order to reduce the chance of loss. These **risk management techniques** include:

1. **Avoidance** – risk avoidance involves staying away from activity that may increase the chance for loss, such as taking a cab instead of getting behind the wheel of car when drinking.
2. **Reduction** – risk reduction is affirmative action taken to reduce the potential for loss occurring, such as equipment inspections and installation of a fire suppression system.

3. **Retention** – with risk retention, an insured may hold back some of the cost associated with a loss, such as the case with selecting a large deductible.
4. **Sharing** – risk sharing is the act of sharing loss among a large risk pool such as a risk retention group.
5. **Transfer** – risk transfer is the act of purchasing insurance in order to transfer the financial impact of the loss to the insurer.

Law of Large Numbers

The **law of large numbers** is a key concept for insurance companies. As one of the elements of an ideal risk, it is predicated on approximating the probability of a loss occurring by increasing the size of the group exposed. The larger the group, the closer the loss will be equal to its probability of occurring.

Insurance

Insurance is a form of risk transfer between an insurance company and the insured for the protection against a reduction in value due to a loss. The contract is an **aleatory contract**, where an unequal exchange of value exists between the owner of the policy (small premium amount) and the insurance company issuing the policy (large potential benefit). It is also considered a contract of **indemnity**, restoring a person to their original value after suffering a loss (pure risk –"*loss only, no gain*")

Insurable Interest

In order for a person to receive the proceeds of an insurance policy after experiencing a loss, there must exist an **insurable interest** between the claimant and the property that suffered the loss. Insurable interest can be the interests of the insured and any legal or financial relationship to the property, rights of ownership, contractual rights and legal liability associated with the loss.

Types of Insurers

An insurer is the party that issues the insurance policy that protects against the potential for financial hardship due to loss. There are several different types of insurers:

- **Stock Companies** – stock companies are a type of insurance company that are publicly-traded companies owned by shareholders.
- **Mutual Companies** – a mutual company differs from a stock company in that there are no shareholders. The company is owned by its policy owners, who receive dividends, which represent the unearned portion of their premiums paid, which have been returned to them by the insurance company.
- **Reciprocal Companies** – a reciprocal company is an unincorporated entity established by group members who are managed by an **attorney-in-fact**. The members of the exchange are known as subscribers who pay premiums to a pool. If the premiums paid are not sufficient to pay claims, an additional premium assessment is made.

- **Lloyd's of London** – this group is similar to a reciprocal group, whereby it is made up of a group of syndicates who specialized in unique risk. The risks assumed by any member of the group syndicate becomes their liability.
- **Fraternal Benefit Societies** – a fraternal benefit society is a type of organization organized as a non-profit association. They provide benefits for individuals that are members of the society, typically lodges, religious orders or charitable benefit societies.
- **Risk Retention Groups** – a risk retention group is a type of insurer that spreads risks among members who are responsible for their pro-rata share of a potential loss. Each of the members of the group brings with it a large number of insurable units that are homogenous in nature.

Domicile of the Insurance Company

An insurance company can be one of the following types in terms of its *domicile* (location) relative to the state in which it is doing business in: **domestic** (headquartered in the state), **foreign** (headquartered in another state), or **alien** (headquartered in another country).

Admitted vs. Non-Admitted

An insurer that is **admitted** has been issued a **Certificate of Authority** by a state's commissioner of insurance and is authorized to transact business. An admitted insurer may be a domestic, foreign or alien domiciled insurer. A **non-admitted** insurer is one who is not authorized to transact business in the state nor has it been issued a Certificate of Authority. Such an insurer works with a **surplus lines broker** (see below).

Producers (Agents, Brokers and Consultants)

Individuals who work with an insurance company to transact business may be an **agent**, **broker** or **consultant**. An insurance agent is contracted directly to the insurer and represents the interests of the company. Such an individual may be considered **exclusive** or **captive**, and only permitted to sell the products offered by the company in which they are contracted with. A **broker (independent agent)** is an individual who may represent more than one insurance company and represents the interests of the insured, not the insurance company. A consultant is a type of licensee that provides insurance advice to clients for which they may be permitted to charge a fee.

Surplus Lines Broker

A **surplus lines broker** is a type of producer who is *licensed* and permitted to work on the behalf of a *non-admitted* insurer. The type of business transacted through surplus lines may be of amounts or types that are unobtainable through a traditional carrier (i.e. Lloyds of London). Each state regulates the licensing and activity of surplus lines and their brokers.

Producer Duties and Responsibilities

A producer's authority comes from the insurer. The type of relationship that a producer has with the insurer, whether as an exclusive or independent agent, dictates how products can be represented and the extent to which the insurer (as **principal**) is bound to the terms of the contract.

The chief responsibilities that a producer has to the insurer include:

1. Fiduciary duty to collect premiums, keep them segregated from personal accounts and remit them promptly to the insurer.
2. Provide the insurer with all material facts that affect the insurer's decision to continue coverage.
3. Make product recommendations to customers that are suitable to their needs.

Law of Agency

The **law of agency** holds that the producer as *agent* acts on the behalf of the insurer, who is the *principal*. The actions of the agent bind the obligations of the principal.

Types of Authority

The agent is given authority to act for the principal. There are three types of authority that are derived from the agent – principal relationship:

- **Expressed** Authority – the authority given to the agent by the principal that is written in the contract.
- **Implied** Authority – a type of authority that the public assumes the agent has, such as taken an application from a customer or collection initial premium payments.
- **Apparent** Authority – authority that exceeds what is given to the agent by their actions (this type of authority is not permitted). An example of apparent authority is an agent accepting payments for a policy and depositing them into their personal checking account.

Concept Review

Insurance is based on insuring **risks**. A risk is defined as a *chance for loss*. Of the two types of risks, **speculative** risks (chance for loss or gain) and **pure** risks (chance for loss only, no gain), only pure risks are covered by insurance. A risk is created by a cause, known as a **peril**, which increases the possibility of a loss occurring. Perils are increased by conditions or actions called a **hazard**. The three types of hazards are: (1) **physical**, which are environmental hazards; (2) **moral**, which is an act that may be deceptive or dishonest; and, (3) **morale**, which is a state of indifference or ignorance.

There are conditions that a *pure risk* must meet in order to be considered insurable by an insurance company (*insurer*). These **elements of an ideal insurable risk** include:

1. Risk spread among a large group of unrelated (homogenous) units.
2. Risk must be certain.
3. Risk must be accidental by nature.
4. Risk must create financial hardship.
5. The cost of the risk must be calculable and premium affordable.
6. Risk may not be caused by catastrophic perils.

The selection of risks that are more prone to loss, resulting in more uninsurable individuals to obtain insurance to the detriment of those who are insurable, is known as **adverse selection**. An insurer may reduce the impact of adverse selection through various **risk management** techniques. They include:

1. **Risk Avoidance** – avoiding situations that may increase the chance for loss.
2. **Risk Reduction** – engaging in preventative or reduction strategies to lessen the impact of loss.
3. **Risk Retention** – retaining a portion of the cost of a potential loss.
4. **Risk Sharing** – spreading the risk of loss through a risk pool of similar units.
5. **Risk Transfer** – purchasing insurance.

Approximating the potential value of a loss done through the observation of risk within a large group of units that are similar in nature (homogenous). This is known as the **Law of Large Numbers**.

Insurance must be based on an **insurable interest** between the owner of the insurance policy and the item being insured. It is assumed in property and casualty insurance that the owner of a business, home or auto has an *insurable interest* in the property rights or for claims arising from personal or professional liability. Insurance policies are issued by different types of insurance companies, which include:

- **Stock Companies** – a type of insurance company owned by shareholders.
- **Mutual Companies** – a type of insurance company owned by its policy owners.
- **Reciprocal Companies** – a type of insurance company that is an unincorporated entity managed by an "**attorney-in-fact**."
- **Lloyds of London** – a type of insurance company that specializes in unique types of risk not normally placed by traditional insurance companies.
- **Fraternal Benefit Societies** – a type of insurance company who sells it policies to members of a lodge, religious order or other benefit society.
- **Risk Retention Groups** – a type of insurance company that spreads risk among its members on a pro-rata basis. Each of the members brings a share of large, homogenous units to the group for the purpose of insurance.

An insurance company doing business in a state in which it is headquartered is considered to be a **domestic** insurer; a company doing business in a state that is headquartered in another state is a **foreign** insurer; a company doing business in a state that is headquartered in another country is an **alien** insurer. An insurer that has been issued a **Certificate of Authority** by the state's insurance commissioner and is authorized to do business is said to be **admitted**. A **non-admitted** insurer is one that has not been issued a Certificate of Authority. A non-admitted insurer offers unique risk through the services of a **surplus lines broker**.

The business of an insurer is transacted through a licensed **agent** or **broker**. An *agent*, which may be **exclusive** or **captive**, represents the interest of the insurance company (in accordance with the **Laws of Agency**). Under the *Laws of Agency*, the *agent* has a **fiduciary responsibility** to the insurer to act financially (such as collecting premiums). A broker (also referred to as an **independent agent**) is licensed to sell on the behalf of several insurers. A broker represents the interest of the consumer in an insurance transaction.

An agent that is contracted to an insurance company is permitted certain **authority** in its relationship as agent – **principal** (insurer). These include:

- **Expressed** Authority – authority granted to the agent by the contract between the parties.
- **Implied** Authority – authority the public assumes the agent holds when acting for the principal, which includes taking applications and collecting initial premiums.
- **Apparent** Authority – authority that exceeds expressed and implied authority given to the agent.

Key Definitions

TERM	DEFINITION
Admitted	A company that has been issued a Certificate of Authority and is authorized to do business in the state.

TERM	DEFINITION
Adverse Selection	The likelihood that those who are uninsurable obtain insurance to the detriment of those who are insurable and considered to be ideal insurance risks.
Agent	A licensed individual who represents the interests of the insurer.
Alien Insurer	An insurance company doing business in a state that is domiciled in another country.
Apparent Authority	Authority exceeding an agent's expressed or implied authority.
Attorney-in-Fact	Individual who manages the affairs of a reciprocal company, including the collection of premium assessments.
Broker	A licensed individual who represents the interests of the consumer.
Certificate of Authority	Authorization to do business in a state issued by a state department of insurance or insurance commission.
Domestic Insurer	An insurance company doing business in a state that is domiciled in the same state.
Expressed Authority	Authority permitted to an agent under the contract.
Fiduciary Responsibility	The responsibility of an agent to act in financial transactions for the insurer, such as collecting premiums.
Foreign Insurer	An insurance company doing business in a state that is domiciled in another state.
Fraternal Benefit Societies	A type of insurance company that insures risks of its members, such as those belonging to a fraternal order or society, religious order or other benefit society or lodge.
Hazard	Increases the likelihood of a peril resulting in risk.
Implied Authority	Authority the public assumes an agent has, such as collecting initial premium payments.
Insurable Interest	The relationship between the insured and the potential for loss covered by insurance.

TERM	DEFINITION
Law of Agency	The relationship between an agent and the insurance company acting as principal, for the agent to act on its behalf.
Law of Large Numbers	The predictability of loss as observed in a large group of homogenous units.
Lloyds of London	A type of insurance company that insures specialized and unique types of risks.
Moral Hazard	An act of dishonesty or fraud that leads to peril.
Morale Hazard	Indifference or ignorance of a standard of conduct or law that increases peril.
Mutual Companies	A type of insurance company that is owned by policy owners. Pays policy dividends.
Non-Admitted	A company doing business in a state that has not been issued a Certificate of Authority. Lines of business are sold through a surplus lines broker.
Peril	A situation that increase the presence of a risk (i.e. lightning, fire, etc.)
Physical Hazard	A condition in the environment that contributes to a peril.
Pure Risk	Risks that result in the chance for loss only and no possibility of gain.
Reciprocal Companies	A type of insurance company that is made of members who pay an assessment into a risk pool; the group is unincorporated and managed by an attorney-in-fact.
Risk	The possibility for loss to occur.
Risk Avoidance	Avoiding situations that increase the potential for loss.
Risk Management	Techniques used by an insurer to reduce the impact of risk or the potential for loss.
Risk Reduction	Engaging in preventative actions to lessen severity of loss.
Risk Retention	Hold back a portion of the cost of a potential loss (i.e. selecting a deductible).
Risk Retention Group	A type of insurance arrangement made of members who pay premiums on a *pro rata* basis to cover potential loss. Each member brings a large group of homogenous units to the group.

TERM	DEFINITION
Risk Sharing	Spread loss among a group of similar units.
Risk Transfer	Purchase insurance.
Speculative Risk	Risks that result in the possibility of a gain or loss.
Stock Companies	A type of insurance company that is owned by shareholders. Pay stock dividends.
Surplus Lines Broker	A type of licensed agent who sells on the behalf of a non-admitted insurer.

Chapter Questions

1. All of the following are types of agent authority, EXCEPT:
   A. Apparent
   B. Implied
   C. Direct
   D. Expressed

2. Which of the following is an example of risk retention?
   A. Purchasing homeowner's insurance
   B. Selecting a large deductible for your personal auto insurance
   C. Spreading the cost of a potential loss with a group of friends
   D. All of the above

3. The type of producer that represents the interest of an individual carrier is known as:
   A. Exclusive agent
   B. Independent agent
   C. Captive agent
   D. A and C only

4. An individual licensed to conduct business on behalf of a non-admitted insurance company is known as:
   A. Broker
   B. Independent agent
   C. Surplus lines broker
   D. Captive agent

5. A membership organization that issues insurance policies is what type of insurer?
   A. Fraternal benefit society
   B. Risk retention group
   C. Mutual insurance company
   D. Stock insurance company

Answer Key

1. The correct answer is **C**. Authority used by an agent when dealing on behalf of an insurance company (acting as principal) include expressed and implied authorities. Authority exceeding expressed and implied authority is known as apparent authority.

2. The correct answer is **B**. Risk retention is defined as retaining a portion of the cost of a potential loss by the insured, such as the selection of a deductible.

3. The correct answer is **D**. An exclusive or captive agent is a type of producer who represents the interests of the insurer, under the laws of agency.

4. The correct answer is **C**. A surplus lines broker is permitted to offer coverages for special risk protection from non-admitted insurers.

5. The correct answer is **A**. Insurance coverage provided to individuals that belong to a benefit society, religious order or other mutual benefit organization is done through a fraternal benefit society.

INSURANCE BASICS

Continuing on with general and basic concepts concerning insurance, here are some basics that you will be tested on. They include management structures, how insurance is marketed and sold to consumers, how risk is selected and underwritten, mandatory and optional provisions of the insurance policy, and legal considerations.

Functions of the Insurance Company

It is important to understand how insurance companies operate and function. There are three main operational functions of any insurance: **actuarial**, **sales & marketing**, and **underwriting**. Each of these areas is directly involved in the selection, classification and acceptance of risk on behalf of the insurance company.

- *Actuarial* departments are involved in the setting of rates for the insurance company. Actuaries are individuals who analyze statistical tables in order to properly assess the probability of loss for an insurance company.
- *Sales & marketing* functions are responsible for the distribution of products offered by the insurance company. A company's sales force selects prospective risk, provides rate illustrations, prepares applications, collects initial premiums and delivers the issued policy.
- *Underwriting* functions as the risk selection arm of the insurance company. An underwriter's job is to assess the potential risk presented in the application submitted by the company's sales representatives (*agents* and *brokers*) and apply the appropriate risk factors and ratings, as well as guard against *adverse selection*.

The Insurance Policy

The **policy** represents an agreement between the insurer and the policy holder (owner) to provide a benefit in the event of a loss. There are different parts to the policy and the policy application that an agent needs to understand.

Application

Before an insurance policy can be issued for a covered risk, information must be gathered by an insurance agent and presented to the company's underwriting unit. The **application** form for most types of property and casualty (and liability) insurance is similar to the sample below (Figure 2):

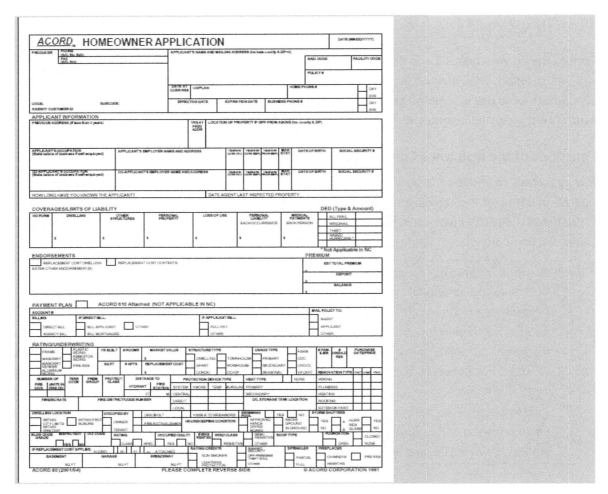

Figure 2 Sample Accord Homeowner's Insurance Policy Application

Types of Receipts

Once the application has been written, coverage may be bound by the agent on behalf of the insurer. This is accomplished through the issuance of a receipt. The three types of common receipts issued by an agent include:

- **Conditional** Receipt – once the initial premium is paid, the date of effective coverage will be the date of the application, unless the application is declined.
- **Unconditional** Receipt – upon receipt of the initial premium, effective coverage begins immediately for a fixed period of time, regardless of acceptance of the application by the insurer (also referred to as the *temporary insurance agreement*).
- **Acceptance** Receipt – the effective date of coverage is the same as the application approval date.

Reinsurance

Reinsurance is a process where risk beyond a company's retention limit (the amount of loss that is in excess of what the insurance company is willing to accept on a case-by-case basis) is shared with another insurance company or a group of insurers. The members of a group in this risk-sharing arrangement are referred to as a syndicate, and the individual companies are known as **reinsurers**. Reinsurance is written under an agreement whereby the company where the risk originates (**ceding company**) "cedes" the excess risk to other insurance companies that are part of the syndicate. There

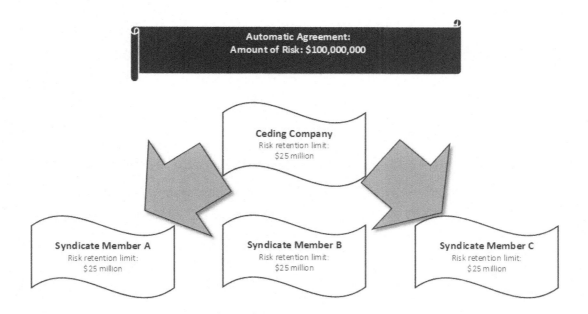

Figure 3 Illustration of an Automatic Agreement Reinsurance Arrangement

are two types of reinsurance arrangements: **automatic** and **facultative** (Figures 3 and 4).

In an *automatic agreement*, the excess risk is ceded to members of the syndicate with no consultation.

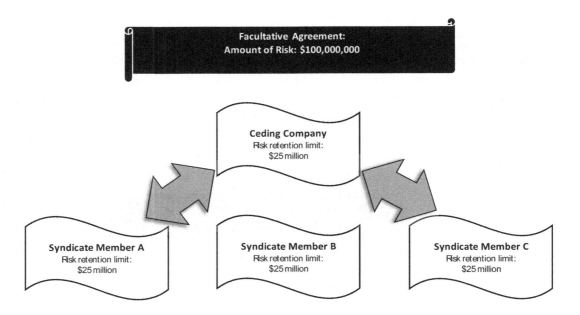

Figure 4 Illustration of a Facultative Agreement Reinsurance Arrangement

In a *facultative agreement*, the excess risk ceded to the members of the syndicate may be re-underwritten and, if necessary, additional conditions may be attached to the final policy issued by the ceding company.

Policy Ratings

Information concerning rates for property and casualty types of insurance come from data compiled for insurers by actuaries through the **Insurance Services Office** (ISO), based in Washington, D.C. ISO rate-making services for property and casualty insurance issuers include the following lines of coverage: Business Owners; Commercial Automobile; Commercial General Liability; Commercial Inland Marine; Commercial Package Policy; Commercial Property; Commercial Umbrella; Crime and Fidelity; Homeowners; and, Personal Auto insurance.

Mandatory (Standard) Policy Provisions

The issued policy includes certain provisions that are required by state law. These provisions, known as **mandatory or standard policy provisions**, protect the interests of the policy owner. These provisions include: entire contract, incontestability period, grace period, reinstatement period, notice of claims, claim forms, proof of loss, time payment of claims and legal actions.

Entire Contract

The **entire contract** provision holds that an issued policy must include the policy form, any conditions, amendments, riders and a copy of the application.

Incontestability Clause

The **incontestability clause** is the period of time in which the insurance company may challenge any material misstatement made at the time of application. This period is typically two years.

Grace Period

The **grace period** is the amount of time that policy premiums may go unpaid before coverage lapses. This period may be 30 or 31 days, depending on the state where the policy was issued.

Reinstatement

The **reinstatement** period is a period of time after the grace period when a policy holder may reinstate coverage that was previously in force. The reinstatement process involves the payment of any premiums in arrears, as well as proof of insurability.

Notice of Claim

The **notice of claim** is a process by which the insured informs the insurer that a loss has occurred.

Claim Forms

Claim forms are a document required by an insurer that provides information on the loss that occurred.

Proof of Loss

Proof of loss is a form provided by the insured to the insurer that demonstrates that a loss has occurred. A form of proof of loss may be a medical bill or statement, accident, police or damage report.

Time Payment of Claims

Under the **time payment of claims** provision in the contract, an insurance company is required to make timely payments on claims presented, provided that such claims follow the form established by the insurer.

Legal Actions

If the insured believes that a claim was improperly handled (usually upon the declination of a claim), they are given the right to file **legal actions** against the insurer, after waiting a period of 60 days from the date the claim was declined. The insured has up to 3 years after the 60 day period in which to file *legal action* against the insurer.

Optional Policy Provisions

In addition to those policy provisions required by law to be contained in the insurance contract, the insurer may also include certain **optional policy provisions**. The purpose of *optional policy provisions* is to protect the interest of the insurer.

Misstatement of Age or Gender

The **misstatement of age or gender** provision allows an insurer to make an adjustment to a policy's premium based on incorrect information provided on the policy application. This provision adjusts the premium rate charged higher for lower ages reported or provides for a refund of premiums charged for a higher age recorded on the application. Regarding the misstatement of gender, a premium adjustment would be made relevant to the gender of the insured (important for auto insurance). This provision allows an adjustment to be made without having to invoke the incontestability clause.

Other Insurance with this Insurer

The **other insurance with this insurer** provision prevents over-insurance from occurring. The provision permits the policy owner to designate one of the policies as primary coverage. The insurer will return premiums paid for the excess coverage.

Insurance with Other Insurers

The **insurance with other insurer's** provision permits a policy owner to select between either insurance company's coverage as the primary policy. Benefits not payable under the primary policy may be assigned to the other insurer's policy.

Unpaid Premiums

Unpaid premiums may cause a policy owner's policy lapse. An insurer offers a **grace period** for a policy owner (30 or 31 days) to pay premiums before the policy lapses. If a loss occurs during the grace period, a benefit will be paid pursuant to any claim, less the amount of premium outstanding.

Conformity with State Statutes

The **conformity with state statutes** provision of the contract is required when an insurer includes any of the optional provisions. It is a statement that affirms that the inclusion of any optional provision conform to the statutes of the state in which the policy is being issued.

Illegal Act

The **illegal act** provisions provides an exclusion from coverage for certain acts that are deemed illegal (i.e. fraud, theft, etc.). Such acts may also be considered a *moral hazard.*

Intoxicants and Narcotics

An optional policy provision regarding **intoxicants and narcotics** provides an exclusion for the insurer from covering losses that result from the use of a drugs and alcohol. The provision may also be referred to as a substance abuse exclusion.

Cancellation

An optional policy provision that permits an insurer to cancel coverage for a stated reason (other than nonpayment of premiums) through a **notice of cancellation**. Such a notice may be required to be given to a policy owner within 30 days of cancellation and in some states up to 60 days. Some jurisdictions may also require and advanced *notice of cancellation* take place between 10 to 75 days. It may also be referred to as a *nonrenewal clause*.

Legal Considerations

The insurance policy represents a legal contract between two specific parties, the *insurer*, who issues the policy and the *policy owner* to whom all rights are conferred. The policy is based on the *insurable interest* of the owner against the risk arising from a loss occurring.

For the contract to be considered legally binding between the parties, there are five elements that must be present (the absence of any which may result in the policy being considered void). These elements are **offer**, **consideration**, **acceptance**, **legal competence** of all parties and **legal purpose** for the contract.

Offer, Consideration, Acceptance

An *offer* is represented by the payment of an initial premium payment. *Consideration* takes place when a completed application is submitted to the insurance company, while the issued policy represents *acceptance*.

Legal Competence

A person deemed mentally incapacitated or unable to understand the terms of a legal contract would lack the *legal competence* necessary to enter into an agreement for insurance. This includes individuals who have not met the age of majority in the state in which the insurance policy will be issued.

Legal Purpose

A contract must be for a *legal purpose* in order to be considered legally binding. For example, a contract to import illegal drugs from another country would not be legally enforceable in a civil court for breach of contract, even if the parties to the contract possessed competence and an offer, consideration and acceptance took place. Such a contract lacks legal purpose and would be unenforceable.

Representations and Warranties

Statements made during the application process by a proposed insured provide the insurer with a basis for issuing the policy of coverage. Two types of common statements made are **representations** and **warranties**.

- *Representations* – a representation is a statement made that an individual believes to be true and factual at the time the statement is made. As an example, an individual who is a man makes a representation that they are a male when checking such a box on an application for insurance.
- *Warranties* – a warranty is a statement that is a guaranteed representation. It differs from a representation in that if such a statement were found out to be untrue at some later time, it may serve as the basis for voiding the policy.

Misrepresentation, Concealment and Fraud

In addition to *representations* and *warranties*, other types of statements and actions taken by the *applicant* (typically the person applying for the coverage and may in many cases be the insured and the owner of the policy) may be taken that could cause the policy to be void, cancelled or legal action to be taken. These types of statement and/or actions include **misrepresentation**, **concealment** and **fraud**.

- *Misrepresentation* refers to a statement made at the time of application that is false. If such a statement were important in the insurer's consideration and acceptance of risk (deemed material), the policy may be voided.
- *Concealment* is the withholding of material facts for the purpose of obtaining insurance.
- *Fraud* takes misrepresentation and concealment one step further in that is intentional for the sole purpose of not only hiding material facts that would influence the insurer's decision to issue the policy, but also to cause harm or injury (with respect to insurance, to receive benefits for a claim).

Legal Interpretations Regarding a Contract of Insurance

There exists legal considerations regarding insurance include those regarding the type of agreement between the parties. The enforcement of a contract of insurance falls under **contract** law and **tort** law (the infliction of injurious harm by one party onto another party).

- **Contract of Adhesion** is a type of contract whereby one party (insurer) prepares the terms and conditions of the contract, presenting them to the other party (insured) on an "all-or-none" (AON) basis.
- **Aleatory contract** is a type of contract where an unequal exchange of value exists. In the case of insurance, the policy owner pays a small premium amount in relationship to the potential value of a loss, should it occur.
- **Conditional contract** is a type of contract that imposes duties on the parties in the contract. The condition for the policy owner is to pay premiums as scheduled and the condition imposed on the insurer is to pay claims when presented with notification and proof of loss.
- **Contract of Indemnity** is a type of contract where by an insured is restored to the original value of the loss, with no gain or profit (hence covering the *pure risk* of the insured).

- **Personal contract** is a type of contract that provides coverage for the insurable interest of the person insured; the rights conferred upon the insurable interest of the insured are not transferrable to another party.
- **Unilateral contract** is a type of contract that legally binds the insurer to the terms of the contract, provided that premiums are paid by the insured (policy owner).

Further, when considering a contract entered into between two or multiple parties, there are some legal interpretations that affect how a court may view the contract. These interpretations include:

- **Ambiguities in a Contract of Adhesion** – because the terms and conditions of the contract are written by the insurer and presented to the insured on an AON basis, confusions or ambiguity on the part of the non-drafting party go against the drafting party.
- **A contract of utmost good faith** – it is expected that both parties entering into agreement do so on the basis of statements and promises made in good faith.

Waiver and Estoppel

A **waiver** is the voluntary abandonment of a legal right known to the party making the waiver. **Estoppel** refers to stopping action or the denial of a fact, if such fact was accepted by prior action of a party. If an individual has consistently made premium payments 1-2 days after the grace period and the insurer consistently accepts those payments, *estoppel* would prevent the insurer from cancelling coverage for nonpayment as the individual has relied on this fact to make premium payments.

Concept Review

The insurance company has several operational functions that are important to the issuance of an insurance policy. Three of the main areas include **actuarial**, **sales & marketing** department and **underwriting**. The *actuarial* department is involved in the setting of rates for the insurer based on company experience and the similar risk experience of other insurance companies. *Sales & marketing* engages in the placement of risk through the advertising and sales of products issued by the insurer. Finally the *underwriting* department's responsibility is the selection of risk based on certain risk factors and a classification system for rating risk. Another function of the underwriters is to protect against **adverse selection**, which is the preponderance of individuals with a greater probability of loss buying insurance to the detriment of those who do not represent a high level of risk to the insurer.

The insurance **policy** is a contract or agreement between the insurance company and the policy holder or owner. The issuance of an insurance *policy* begins with the taking of an **application**, which provides the insurance with necessary information critical for assessing and *underwriting* risk. Completion of the *application* results in the issuance of a **receipt** by the *agent* to the insured. Three types of receipts are: **conditional receipt**, which sets the effective date of coverage as the date of application upon receipt of the initial premium, unless the application is declined; **unconditional receipt**, which starts the coverage period immediately upon receipt of the initial premium for a fixed period, regardless of acceptance of the risk by the insurer. This is also referred to as a **temporary insurance agreement.** Lastly, the **acceptance receipt** sets the application date as the approval date upon receipt of the initial premium and acceptance of the risk by the insurer.

In the case where the amount of risk presented to the insurer is more than the amount that the company is permitted to retain for an individual case, a process known as **reinsurance** takes place. *Reinsurance* involves the placement of excess risk beyond an insurer's retention limit with another insurer known as a **reinsurer** or group of insurers as part of an **underwriting syndicate**. *Reinsurance* takes place under either an **automatic agreement**, whereby the company in which the risk originates (**ceding company**) cedes the excess risk to the reinsurers or members of the underwriting syndicate who accept the risk as-is. In a **facultative agreement**, the excess risk ceded to the reinsurers may be evaluated by the syndicate members. Conditions or amendments may be added to the final policy issued by the group. Insurance risk is rated by an insurer's underwriters based on data provided by sources such as the **Insurance Services Office** (ISO) based in Washington, D.C.

An issued *policy* contains **provisions** that are either **mandatory** and required by state law or **optional** and included for the protection of the insurer. *Mandatory policy provisions* are mandated and protect the interests of the policy owner. They include entire contract, incontestability period, grace period, reinstatement period, notice of claims, claim forms, proof of loss, time payment of claims and legal actions. *Optional policy provisions*, which protect the interests of the insurance company, may be included as long as a provision called **Conformity with State Laws** is also included, attesting that any optional provision included meets the requirements of the state in which the policy is issued. Optional policy provisions include **misstatement of age or gender**, **other insurance** with this insurer, **insurance with other insurers**, **unpaid premiums**, **illegal acts**, **intoxicants and narcotics**, and notice of **cancellation**.

There are legal considerations taken into account when issuing an insurance policy. These legal considerations involve the parties to the contract: the insurance company as issuer of the policy and the policy owner upon whom all rights of ownership are conferred. The policy is issued on the basis of the owner's **insurable interest**, in that which is being insured against the risk associated with a potential for loss.

A contract of insurance is not considered legally binding if it does not meet each of the following elements: **offer** (initial premium payment), **consideration** (application), **acceptance** (issued policy), **legal competence** of the parties involved and **legal purpose** for the contract (of which insurance meets). Statements made during the application process and relied upon by the insurer in determining the issuance of an insurance policy may be **representations** or **warranties**. **Representations** are statements of fact that are believed to be true at the time they are made. **Warranties** are a guaranteed representation that if found untrue may serve as a basis for the policy becoming void. **Misrepresentations** are statements made that are false. If a *misrepresentation* is deemed to have been material to the insurer's decision in issuing the policy, the policy may be voided. **Concealment** involves the withholding of a material fact. **Fraud** is a step beyond *misrepresentation* and *concealment* as it is an intentional act done to influence a decision about insurance that results in injurious harm.

Insurance policies are contracts that involve both **contract** and **tort law**, which is defined as the infliction of harm by one party on to another party. The contract is considered a: **contract of adhesion**, prepared on an all-or-none basis when presented by the insurer; an **aleatory contract** that constitutes the exchange of unequal values between the insurer and the policy owner; **conditional contract** that imposes certain conditions upon each party; a **contract of indemnity** that provides for the restoration to original value after a loss has been experienced; a **personal contract** that covers the insurable interest of the policy owner; a **unilateral contract** that binds the insurer to meet the terms of the policy provided that premiums are paid. Any ambiguities in a **contract of adhesion** are interpreted in favor of the party that was not involved in drafting the policy. The insurance policy is also considered to be based on a **contract of utmost good faith** between the parties. A right that is given to a party may be abandoned through a process known as **waiver**. If a party has engaged in an action that has been accepted previously as a fact, that party is prevented from later denying such fact through the concept of **estoppel**.

Key Definitions

TERM	DEFINITION
Acceptance	The issuance of an insurance policy by an insurer.
Acceptance Receipt	Sets the effective date of coverage as the application date

TERM	DEFINITION
	upon receipt of the initial premium.
Actuarial Department	The function area responsible for rate setting.
Application	The form that provides the insurer with information necessary to assess risk.
Automatic Agreement	A type of reinsurance arrangement where risk is ceded to members of an underwriting syndicate. Upon acceptance of that risk, no further consultation takes place.
Ceding Company	The company where risk originates for reinsurer.
Claim Forms	The form in which a loss must be reported to the insurer by the insured.
Concealment	The intentional withholding of facts that may have had an impact on an insurer's decision to issue a policy.
Conditional Receipt	A receipt that establishes the application date as date of coverage upon acceptance of risk by the insurer.
Conformity with State Statutes	Any optional provision that requires any optional policy provision included to conform to the laws of the state in which the policy is issued.
Consideration	The application form for insurance coverage.
Entire Contract	Includes the issued policy, amendments, riders and the application for insurance.
Estoppel	Prohibits the denial of an omitted fact if accepted by a prior action.
Facultative Agreement	A type of reinsurance arrangement where risk is ceded to members of an underwriting syndicate. Members of the syndicate may consult with the ceding company concerning the risk and make amendments to the policy.

TERM	DEFINITION
Fraud	An intentional act to hide a material fact through misrepresentation, concealment, deceit or fraud. Such an act has an intent to cause harm or injury, resulting in a loss.
Grace Period	The period of time, 30 or 31 days, which the policy owner has to remit unpaid premiums before coverage lapses.
Illegal Act	Any act consisting including fraud, deceit, theft, etc. that may exclude the payment of policy benefits.
Incontestability Clause	The period of time, usually 2 years, that an insurer has to challenge any material misstatements made on the application.
Insurance Service Office (ISO)	A provider of rate making data for property & casualty insurers based in Washington, D.C.
Insurance with Other Insurers	Requires the insured to designate a policy owned with the either insurer as primary for the payment of a claim. Any excess amount not covered by the primary policy may be applied to a secondary policy owned with the other insurer.
Intoxicants and Narcotics	A provision that provides an exclusion of benefits if the cause of the loss was based on the use of intoxicants and narcotics such as alcohol and illicit drugs.
Legal Competence	An element of a legal contract that requires all parties to be deemed competent to enter into the agreement.
Legal Purpose	An element of a legal contract that requires that the purpose of the contract be legal.
Mandatory Policy Provisions	Policy provisions required in an insurance contract for the protection of the policy owner.
Misrepresentation	A false statement made in the application.
Misstatement of Age or Gender	May affect benefits payable for medical related policies; will result in a premium adjustment.

TERM	DEFINITION
Notice of Cancellation	A notice provided to a policy owner for a stated reason (other than non-payment of premiums). May also be referred to as a nonrenewal notice.
Notice of Claim	The period of time an insured is required to notify the insurer that a loss has occurred.
Offer	The payment of an initial premium.
Optional Policy Provisions	Policy provisions that may be included by the insurer for their protection. The inclusion of any optional policy provisions must include the conformity with state laws provision.
Other Insurance with this Insurer	Requires the insured to designate a policy owned with the same insurer as primary for the payment of a claim. Any premiums paid for excess coverage will be returned in order to prevent over-insurance.
Policy	An agreement between the insurer and the policy holder to provide benefits in the event that a loss occurs.
Reinsurance	The ceding of risk from one insurance company to another.
Reinsurers	An individual company that is a member of an underwriting syndicate.
Representations	Statements made in the application, believed to be true to the best knowledge of the individual making the statement.
Sales & Marketing	The function area responsible for advertising and selling insurance products.
Time Payment of Claims	The period of time that the insured has to pay benefits on a claim based on receipt of all required forms.
Unconditional Receipt	A receipt that establishes coverage immediately upon receipt of the premium for a fixed period of time, regardless if the policy is issued. Also known as the temporary

TERM	DEFINITION
	insurance agreement.
Underwriting	The function area responsible for risk selection.
Waiver	The abandonment of a known right.
Warranties	A guaranteed representation that, if proven false, may result in the insurance policy becoming void.

Chapter Questions

1. The period of time an insurer may challenge any material misstatement on the application is known as:
   A. Entire Contract
   B. Incontestability
   C. Grace Period
   D. Legal Action

2. What interests are protected by optional policy provisions included in the contract?
   A. Insured
   B. Insurer
   C. Policy owner
   D. Both B and C

3. Which mandatory policy provision prevents over-insurance from occurring?
   A. Other Insurance with this Insurer
   B. Insurance with Other Insurers
   C. Misstatement of Age or Gender
   D. None of the above

4. What is the number of days an insurer must provide to the policy owner concerning the cancellation of a policy (for reasons other than non-payment of policy premiums)?
   A. 10 days
   B. 30 days
   C. 60 days
   D. B and C only

5. Each of the following are elements of a legally binding contract, EXCEPT:
   A. Legal intent
   B. Legal purpose
   C. Acceptance
   D. Consideration

Answer Key

1. The correct answer is **B**. The incontestability period is the period of time an insurance company can challenge a material misstatement made on the application; this period is usually 2 years from the date of application.

2. The correct answer is **B**. Optional policy provisions included in the contract protect the interest of the insurance company.

3. The correct answer is **D**. Choices A, B and C are optional policy provisions, *not* mandatory policy provisions.

4. The correct answer is **D**. An insurer, under the optional policy provision for cancellation/nonrenewal, may be required to provide no less than 30 and up to 60 days notification of their intent to cancel coverage (for reasons other than non-payment of premiums), depending upon the laws of the state in which the policy was issued.

5. The correct answer is **A**. The five elements of a legally binding contract are offer, consideration, acceptance, legal competence of the parties entering into the contract and legal purpose.

PROPERTY INSURANCE BASICS

This chapter will discuss the basic concepts related to **property insurance** (i.e. coverage, loss valuation, insuring methods and common property policy provisions).

Different Property Losses

Property losses are categorized as being either **direct loss** or **indirect loss**. A *direct loss* is defined as being the primary loss or direct damage that is caused as a result of damage regardless of the presence of an intervening cause for the loss. A home damaged by fire of an indeterminate cause or water damage from a pipe that bursts due to extreme cold may be examples of direct loss. An *indirect loss* is the secondary or additional loss that occurs as a result of the direct loss. An example of indirect loss would be if a house fire required an insured family to become displaced and incur the cost of an extended stay at a hotel while the insurance company worked to pay out their claim.

Types of Peril

Perils are the cause for a *loss*. In terms of property insurance, coverage for perils can be a **named peril**, which is specifically expressed in the policy, or an **open peril**, which is coverage for losses caused by any type of peril other than those that are specifically excluded from coverage in the policy. An *open perils* policy may also be referred as a **special form policy**.

Loss Valuation for a Property Insurance Policy

As a *contract of indemnity*, an insurance policy restores the insured to their previous financial condition following a loss. For insurance policies like life or health insurance, loss is valued based on future income potential or the cost of medical assistance. In terms of property insurance, there are different methods that may be used to value a loss.

- **Actual Cash Value** (ACV) – this method covers the replacement value of a covered property, less depreciation costs.
- **Replacement Value** – this method covers the value of replacing an item at current cost, without respect to depreciation and reasonable wear and tear. The insured may be required to cover no more than 80 percent of the replacement value of the covered property so not to over-insure in the event of a partial loss.
- **Stated or Agreed Value** – this method is based on a negotiated cost for a covered property that is paid upon loss, regardless of the actual cost of replacement. A property insurance policy that uses a stated or agreed value method may be providing coverage for rare items such as antique furniture.
- **Valued Policy** – this method provides a stated amount that is expressed in the Declaration page of the policy for covered items subject to a total loss.

Coverage Limits

Coverage limits in a property insurance policy may be accomplished through one of three types (Figure 5): **specific**, **scheduled** and **blanket** coverage limits. A policy using a *specific* coverage limit provides coverage for a single item up to a stated coverage limit. In the example illustrated in Figure 5, a maximum coverage limit of $500,000 applies to the home depicted for a covered loss. A *scheduled limit* provides a maximum limit per item covered in the policy. In the illustration, both property item A and B are covered with each item having its own limit of $500,000. *Blanket* coverage combines the per item coverage limit into an aggregate amount, which represents the total coverage for the policy.

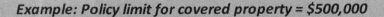

Example: Policy limit for covered property = $500,000

Special limit insuring method - provides an amount of coverage up to the policy limit for a single item. In this example, the coverage is $500,000 for the item depicted.

Example: Policy limit per covered property = $500,000

A   B

   ,

Scheduled limit insuring method - provides coverage for multiple items under a single policy; limits are set per item and may be for different amounts.

Example: Policy limit per covered property = $500,000; Total policy limit = $1,000,000

A   B

   +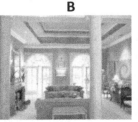

Blanket limit insuring method - provides coverage for multiple items under a single policy with a total (aggregate) limit of coverage.

Figure 5: Coverage limits types for Property Insurance

The Property Insurance Policy

In addition to the policy provisions and legal considerations for insurance policies discussed previously, there are some additional considerations to discuss regarding property insurance policies.

> **Declaration page** – a part of the issued policy that provides the policy owner with information that answers the following questions:
>
> 1. Who are the named parties to the insurance policy (insurer and insured/person)?
>
> 2. What property is covered by the policy?
>
> 3. Where are the insured and the covered property located?
>
> 4. When is the policy effective and when does the policy expire?
>
> 5. How much coverage is provided for the policy, using either a specified, scheduled, or blanket coverage limit, how much are the premiums and how much is the self-insurance (*risk retention*) in the form of a deductible?
>
> **Insuring Agreement** – the insuring agreement provides information on the coverage and what the insurance company will pay in the event that a loss occurs, as effected by any **conditions** and/or **exclusions** (see next section) imposed by the insurer.

Be sure that you understand both the declaration page and insuring agreement, as both will appear on the licensing examination.

Conditions and Exclusions

The insurer may also wish to impose certain *conditions* on the policy, as well as loss that may be subject to *exclusions* from coverage. *Conditions* and *exclusions* protect the insurer from *adverse selection.*

Conditions

Conditions imposed on both the insured and the insurer are shared rights and responsibilities with respect to both parties' duties and obligations under the policy. The **policy period** establishes the period of time coverage provided for loss covered under the policy. If an insurer decides to increase the scope of coverage for a policy that is already in existence without a raise in premiums, the *broadened coverage* will apply to all policies of a similar nature under the policy's **liberalization clause**. Benefits ascribed to a named insured may not be transferred or assigned to another party without the consent of the insurer under the **assignment clause**. **Subrogation** is a condition that permits the insurer, under consent of the insured, to recover the amount of the loss from a third-party who may have been the cause of the loss. This condition helps the insurance company bring down the cost of coverage in terms of premiums and its expenses by holding liable the party deemed the loss cause.

Other conditions that may be imposed by the insurer include:

- **Appraisal** – allows the insured or the insurer to request a binding appraisal when the amount of a loss is in dispute. Under this arrangement, both parties pay the cost of hiring an appraiser, and split the cost of an umpire, who mediates between the opposing appraisals.
- **Duties after a loss** – duties after a loss represent the responsibilities of the insured when a loss occurs, which may include notification of the insurer, obtaining an accident or claims investigation, etc.
- **Mortgage clause** – regarding mortgage insurance, the mortgage clause requires the lender to meet the obligations of a borrower if they fail to meet their requirements, such as paying premiums.

Exclusions

Exclusions are specified perils expressed in the policy that coverage will be declined for. These exclusions are generally for perils that may create a catastrophic exposure to risk (i.e. war and acts of war, neglect, loss that may be intentional in nature, etc.).

Concept Review

Losses in property insurance can be categorized as either **direct** loss or **indirect** loss. *Direct* losses are primary losses resulting from direct damage whether an intervening cause for the loss was present or not. An *indirect* loss is one that occurs as a result of a direct loss. Coverage in a property insurance policy is provided for perils that are specifically expressed in the policy known as **named perils** or those that are the cause for a loss other than those specifically excluded in the policy, which are referred to an **open perils** or **special form policy**.

The valuation of a loss in a property insurance policy is done in one of four ways: by **actual cash value (ACV)**, covering the replacement value of damaged property, less depreciation; **replacement value** covering the value of loss at its current cost (a *replacement value* method requires the insured to cover no more than 80 percent of the value to prevent against over-insurance in the event of a partial loss); **stated or agreed value** method, which represents a negotiated cost for the covered property's loss regardless of the actual replacement cost; and the **valued policy** method that sets a statement amount for the loss in the *declaration page* of the policy. Limits on the amount of coverage for a covered property item in the policy can be **specific**, **scheduled** or **blanket** limits. A *specific limit* sets a coverage limit for a single item. A *scheduled limit* sets a maximum per item limit of coverage, with each item having its own limit. *Blanket limit* provides a combined aggregate limit for all items covered in the policy.

Additional considerations in a property insurance policy include the **declaration page** that provides information to the insured about the names of the parties to the contract, the property being covered, the location of the property as well as the insured, the effective and expiration date of the policy and the amount of coverage provided (subject to the stated coverage limit), deductible and premium amount. There is also an **insuring agreement** that provides information on the amount of coverage and what the insurer is obligated to do when a loss occurs, subject to any **conditions** or **exclusions** imposed by the insurer.

Conditions are the rights and responsibilities of the parties in the policy (insurer and insured). These include the **policy period**, which established the period of time in which a loss will be covered under the policy. If during the *policy period* the insurer decides to change the scope of coverage for a policy already in existence and does not increase the premiums **broadened coverage** occurs under the policy's **liberalization clause**. All benefits set forth in the policy may not be transferred by the insured to another party without the consent of the insurer under what is called the **assignment clause**. **Subrogation** permits the insurer to seek recovery of their costs related to a loss from a third party known to be the cause of the loss.

If the insured and insurer dispute the amount of loss, they may request a binding **appraisal**. The *appraisal* requires both parties to hire an appraiser (of which each party is responsible to pay for) and select an **umpire** who mediates between the two sides. There are responsibilities that the insured must fulfill after a loss takes place, which are known as **duties after a loss**, such as notifying the insurer that a loss has occurred, obtaining and submitting any *claim forms*, accident reports and claim investigations as *proof of loss*. A **mortgage clause** provides protection to a lender in the case of a homeowner's policy or mortgage insurance that requires the lender to meet the obligations of the policy in the event that the borrower fails to meet their requirements, such as paying premiums.

Exclusions set forth those perils (as in the case of a *special forms policy*) that will not be covered by the policy if they are the cause for the loss. Common exclusions include losses due to war, or those that are intentional, water damage, etc.

Key Definitions

TERM	DEFINITION
Actual cash value	Covers replacement value of the loss, less depreciation.
Assignment clause	No benefits assigned to a named insured may be assigned to a third party without the consent of the insurer.
Blanket limit	Provides an overall coverage amount, covering loss for multiple items.
Declaration page	Provides information on who the parties are, what is being covered, where the insured and property are located, the effective date of coverage, and how much coverage is provided.
Direct Loss	Primary loss or direct damage that comes from damage that may or may not be from an intervening cause.
Indirect Loss	Secondary or additional loss that is the result of a direct loss.
Insuring agreement	Sets forth the coverage information for the insured as well as what will be paid when a loss occurs, unless impacted by some condition or exclusion.
Liberalization clause	Any enhanced benefits provided in a policy without an increase in premium will be included to any existing, similar policy issued.
Named Peril	Coverage provided for perils specifically named in the policy.
Open Peril	Coverage provided for any type of peril not excluded by the policy; also referred to as a special forms policy.
Policy period	The period in which losses of the insured will be covered.

TERM	DEFINITION
Replacement value	Covers replacement value of loss at current value, without depreciation. Insured may be limited to protecting up to 80% of the value of the loss in order to prevent against over insurance in the case of a partial loss.
Scheduled limit	Provides a maximum coverage amount in a policy on a per item basis.
Specific limit	Provides a maximum coverage amount in a policy covering a single item.
Stated (Agreed) value	A pre-negotiated value for loss, regardless of the actual cost of the loss.
Subrogation	The ability of the insurer, through consent of the insured, to go after a third-party for the recovery of costs due to their role as the cause of the loss.
Valued policy	Provides total coverage value for loss that is expressed in the declaration page of the policy.

Chapter Questions

1. A policy that covers any type of peril that is specifically referenced provides what type of coverage?
   A. Open perils coverage
   B. Named perils coverage
   C. Any perils coverage
   D. Specific perils coverage

2. A property insurance coverage using replacement value as its valuation method may limit the insured to what percentage of the cost to replace damaged property?
   A. 50%
   B. 75%
   C. 80%
   D. 100%

3. All of the following information is included in the Declaration page, EXCEPT:
   A. The insurer's address
   B. Amount of the deductible
   C. Effective date of coverage
   D. Coverage limit

4. Which of the following is NOT a type of coverage limit?
   A. Specific
   B. Special
   C. Scheduled
   D. Blanket

5. What takes place when an insurer chooses to subrogate a property insurance claim?
   I. A third party is held financially liable for the loss.
   II. The insurer takes action against the insured.
   III. The insured gives consent to the insurer for subrogation.
   A. I only
   B. I and II
   C. I, II and III
   D. I and III only

Answer Key

1. The correct answer is **B**. A named perils coverage scope provides benefits for loss caused by those perils that are specifically named in the policy.

2. The correct answer is **C**. Under the replacement value valuation method, an insured may be limited to 80% of the value of the damaged property, to protect against over-insurance in the event of a partial loss.

3. The correct answer is **A**. The Declaration page provides the insured with information concerning the amount of coverage, any deductible amount, location of the covered property and address of the named insured. The insurer's address is not provided in the declaration page of the policy.

4. The correct answer is **A**. The types of coverage limits available in a property insurance policy are special coverage, scheduled coverage and blanket coverage limit.

5. The correct answer is **D**. Under the rights of subrogation, the insurer, with the consent of the insured, seeks to recover the cost associated with a claim that is deemed the fault of a third party who caused the loss.

TYPES OF PROPERTY INSURANCE

Property insurance consists of the types of insurance policies that provide protection from loss for commercial purposes, dwellings, homeowners and the transportation of goods (Inland Marine). These and other types of property insurance policies will be discussed in this chapter.

Commercial Property Insurance

Property insurance coverage provides protection for losses that occur for an insured both personally and commercially. Beginning with **commercial property insurance**, there are different forms of coverage that are available. Coverage forms of commercial property insurance include:

- **Commercial Property Causes of Loss** refers to coverage for a specified cause of loss as stated in the form. There are three types of cause of loss forms: basic, broad and special.
- **Building and Personal Property Coverage** provides coverage for loss resulting in direct damage to buildings, business personal property and personal property of others. The coverage form does not include coverage for liability.
- **Builders Risk Coverage** provides coverage for loss resulting in direct damage to buildings under construction. Covered property under this form include buildings and structures, foundations, fixtures and machinery, equipment and materials and supply used in construction.
- **Earthquake and Volcanic Eruption Endorsement** is an addition attached to any cause of loss form (i.e. *basic*, *broad* and *special causes of loss*) for damage resulting from an earthquake or eruption of a volcano.

Commercial Package Policy

Commercial property insurance coverage forms that combine different coverages under a single package are referred to as a **Commercial Package Policy** (CPP).

A *Commercial Package Policy* is packaged with two basic components: a **Declarations** page and a **Conditions** page. These components are applicable to all of the additional parts that are added or make up the CPP. The optional parts that can be added to CPP are:

- **Buildings and Building Personal Property (BPP)** coverage provides coverage for loss resulting in direct damage to buildings, business personal property and personal property of others. The coverage form does not include coverage for liability.
- **Business Auto (BAP)** coverage provides coverage for loss due to damage and liability caused by a vehicle in use for business purposes. Coverage for auto related businesses (i.e. repair shops and trucking companies) are excluded from this type of coverage.
- **Commercial General Liability (CGL)** coverage (discussed in more detail later in the chapter entitled *Types of Casualty Insurance*) covers claims of liability for bodily injury and property

damage (Coverage Part A) related to the operations of a business, and personal and advertising injury (Coverage Part B).

- **Commercial Crime** coverage provides coverage for a business against loss due to acts of fraud or acts of dishonesty. Types of acts covered under a commercial crime policy include employee theft and dishonesty, computer fraud, kidnap, ransom, etc.
- **Equipment Breakdown** coverage covers loss caused by damage of a mechanical or electrical nature and loss of use of equipment. This coverage also includes revenue lost and extra expenses associated with the loss of use. Equipment breakdown coverage replaces traditional boiler and machinery (BM) insurance coverage.
- **Inland Marine** coverage provides insurance for items shipped via land transportation as well as various items of transportation such as roads and bridges and communication items such as television radio towers. The coverage also provides for legal liability protection for **bailees** (those entrusted with storing, repairing or servicing property). Also referred to as **floater** insurance.
- **Personal and Advertising Injury Liability** coverage is detailed in a later chapter, *Types of Casualty Insurance.* See information for CGL coverage. Offenses covered include false arrest, malicious prosecution, wrongful eviction, slander, libel, violation of a person's rights to privacy, misuse of advertising, and copyright infringement.

Commercial Property Insurance Causes of Loss Form

A **causes of loss** form provides the insured with coverage for a *named peril*, which is the cause for the loss. There are three types of causes of loss forms for commercial property insurance: basic, broad and special.

- **Basic Causes of Loss (ISO CP 10 10)**

The **basic causes of loss** coverage form in a commercial property insurance policy provides coverage for certain *perils* named in the form. The *named perils* covered under the basic causes of loss form are: fire, lightning, explosion, smoke, and windstorm. Other perils that may be covered include loss due to hail, riot and civil commotion, aircraft, vehicles, vandalism, sprinkler leakage, sinkhole collapse, and volcanic action.

- **Broad Causes of Loss (ISO CP 10 20)**

Under the **broad causes of loss** coverage form, coverage is provided for perils in addition to those listed in the *basic causes of loss* form, which include: falling objects; weight of snow, ice, or sleet; water damage and collapse from a specified cause.

- **Special Causes of Loss (ISO CP 10 30)**

The **special causes of loss** form is also known as the *all risks* coverage form because the form provides coverage for all causes of loss except for those that are specifically excluded by the form.

Homeowners' Insurance

Homeowners insurance provides protection for loss caused by damage to the property of the insured, as well as liability coverage for injury or harm to the homeowner or others. Homeowners insurance meets the needs of individual homeowners, owners of condominiums and apartment tenants, depending on the *causes of loss* form.

Causes of Loss Forms of Homeowners Insurance

Similar to what is found with commercial and property insurance, there are causes of loss forms that are associated with Homeowners Insurance. These forms provide specified coverage for *named perils* listed, depending on the form.

- **Homeowners 1, Basic Form (ISO HO 00 01)**

The homeowners insurance **basic causes of loss** coverage form provides coverage for damage to property, personal liability and medical payments to others. This causes of loss form is not widely available in most states, as customers tend to seek broad-based coverage.

- **Homeowners 2, Broad Form (ISO HO 00 02)**

The **broad causes of loss** coverage form for homeowners insurance provides coverage for direct damage to the home as well as coverage for any private structure attached to the property (i.e. garage), personal property at or away from the home and any loss of use.

- **Homeowners 3, Special Form (ISO HO 00 03)**

The **special causes of loss** coverage form provides coverage that is in addition to the broad causes of loss form for homeowners insurance plus additional coverage for *personal liability* and *medical payments to others*. It is the most common form of homeowners insurance.

- **Homeowners 4, Contents Broad Form (ISO HO 00 04)**

A homeowners insurance **contents broad causes of loss** form provides coverage to a tenant for direct damage to personal property based on a broad named perils basis. This form provides both personal liability and medical payments coverage.

- **Homeowners 5, Comprehensive Form (ISO HO 00 05)**

The **comprehensive causes of loss** homeowners insurance form provides coverage in addition to the *special causes of loss form.* It is considered to be the broadest causes of loss coverage form for homeowners, including other structures and personal property.

- **Homeowners 6, Unit Owners Form (ISO HO 00 06)**

The **unit owners causes of loss** form provides coverage for those that own a condominium or interest in the mutual benefit in a cooperative building. The *unit owners causes of loss* form provides the level of coverage for causes of loss that is similar to the Homeowners 3 *special causes of loss policy* form.

- **Homeowners 8, Modified Coverage Form (ISO HO 00 08)**

A **modified coverage causes of loss** form provides coverage for damage to property, *personal liability* and *medical payments to others* for homes that are owner-occupied. Insurance limits are typically equal to the replacement cost of the home, where market value may be less than the replacement cost. Used primarily with older homes or those built with substandard materials.

Dwelling Insurance

Dwelling insurance differs from *homeowners insurance* in that it provides coverage for causes of loss that may not be covered by homeowners insurance. *Dwelling insurance* coverage may be in addition to standard homeowners insurance coverage or as a standalone policy, depending on the insured's needs and insurance requirements. *Dwelling insurance* includes three types of causes of loss forms that are similar to homeowners insurance (i.e. basic, broad, and special).

- **Dwelling Basic Causes of Loss (ISO DP 00 01)**

  The **dwelling insurance basic causes of loss** coverage form provides coverage for damage to dwellings and personal property caused by named perils that include fire, lightning, and explosions (that are internal). Coverage for other perils may be added by endorsement.

- **Dwelling Broad Causes of Loss (ISO DP 00 02)**

  The **dwelling insurance broad causes of loss** coverage form provides coverage for damage to dwellings and personal property that is in addition to the basic dwelling insurance causes of loss form (DP-1).

- **Dwelling Special Causes of Loss (ISO DP 00 03)**

  The **dwelling insurance special causes of loss** form provides coverage for dwellings and structures on an all risks basis and personal property on a broad causes of loss basis.

Inland Marine Insurance

Inland marine insurance provides protection for loss associated with damage to items (goods and merchandise) that are transported over land (and not held at a fixed location). Property is covered on an *open perils* basis, covering all *perils* except for those specifically excluded. Property eligible for coverage under inland marine insurance must meet the following guidelines as established by the National Association of Insurance Commissioners (NAIC – see the chapter entitled *Insurance Regulation*) under the **nationwide marine definition**:

- Must be in transit
- Must be moveable
- Must be related to transportation of communication, or
- Must be in possession of a bailee

The six types of insurable property subject to coverage in accordance with the nationwide marine definition are:

1. Imported goods and merchandise

2. Exported goods and merchandise
3. Domestic shipments and property for sale or consignment while in transit
4. Bridges, tunnels and communication towers (and other instruments of transportation and communication)
5. Property not usually held at a residence (personal property floater)
6. Property related to a business practice or profession.

Inland marine coverage includes various floaters, which is specific coverage for a type of good or merchandise held by a bailee in transit. Common floaters include:

- Accounts Receivable floater
- Builders risk floater
- Commercial articles floater (i.e. fine arts, photographic equipment, musical instruments, etc.)
- Contractor's equipment floater
- Computer systems floater
- Display sign floater
- Equipment dealers floater
- Installation floater
- Jewelry floater
- Valuable papers and records floater

Flood Insurance

Flood insurance provides coverage for direct damage to buildings and their contents within a participating community. The program is guaranteed by the National Flood Insurance Program (NFIP), a federally funded program established in 1968 to make available funds to those communities affected by flooding. Policies are issued by private insurers that are certified to participate in NFIP. NFIP is administered by the Federal Emergency Management Agency (FEMA), which is part of the U.S. Department of Homeland Security.

Concept Review

Property insurance refers to the different types of coverage used for the protection from loss that occurs personally and commercially. *Property insurance* coverage includes loss for **commercial property, dwellings, homeowners, inland marine** and **flood**.

Commercial property insurance provides protection for loss to property owned, operated or controlled by a business. The types of coverage forms available for *commercial property* loss include:

- **Commercial Property Cause of Loss**
- **Building and Personal Property Coverage**
- **Builders Risk Coverage**
- **Earthquake and Volcanic Eruption Endorsement**

When commercial property coverage forms are combined into a single policy, this is known as a **commercial package policy** (CPP). A commercial package policy consists of two basic components: a **declarations** and **conditions** page. In addition to the basic components to a CPP, optional parts that can be added include:

- **Buildings and Buildings Personal Property** (BPP) Coverage that provides for loss resulting from direct damage to buildings, personal property of the business and personal property of others (liability coverage is not included with this coverage form).
- **Business Auto** (BAP) Coverage that provides for damage and liability associated with a vehicle used for business purposes. Coverage for repair shops and trucking companies (involved in the transportation of goods and merchandise) are excluded.
- **Commercial General Liability** (CGL) coverage protects against claims of liability for bodily injury and property damage and personal and advertising injury.
- **Commercial Crime** coverage protects against loss due to acts of dishonesty, theft and fraud (i.e. computer fraud, employee theft and kidnap or ransom).
- **Equipment Breakdown** coverage protects against loss caused by damage of a mechanical or electrical nature or loss of use of the equipment.
- **Inland Marine** coverage provides protection for items (i.e. goods and merchandise) in transit overland. The coverage provides for the legal liability for personnel entrusted with the storage, repair or servicing of property (**bailees**). Specific forms of *inland marine* coverage are known as **floaters**.
- **Personal and Advertising Injury Liability** coverage protects against such acts as false arrest, malicious prosecution, misuse of advertising and copyright infringement.

A **cause of loss** form provides protection for a **named peril**, which is specifically named in the coverage form (as opposed to an **open peril** or *special forms* coverage, which provides protection for all perils except for those that are specifically excluded). The *causes of loss* forms for *commercial property*, *homeowners* and *dwelling* insurance are:

Commercial Property (CP)

Coverage Form	ISO #	Perils Covered
Basic	ISO CP 1010	Named perils: fire, lightning, explosion, smoke, and windstorm. Other perils that may be covered include loss due to hail, riot and civil commotion, aircraft, vehicles, vandalism, sprinkler leakage, sinkhole collapse, and volcanic action.
Broad	ISO CP 1020	Named perils: Basic + falling objects; weight of snow, ice, or sleet; water damage and collapse from a specified cause.
Special	ISO CP 1030	Open perils (most comprehensive coverage available for commercial property).

Homeowners (HO)

Coverage Form	ISO #	Perils Covered
Basic	ISO HO 0001	Named perils: damage to property, personal liability and medical payments to others (Not widely available in all states).
Broad	ISO HO 0002	Named perils: direct damage to the home as well as coverage for any private structure attached to the property (i.e. garage), personal property at or away from the home and any loss of use.
Special	ISO HO 0003	Named perils: Broad + personal liability and medical payments to others (most common HO coverage purchased).
Contents Broad	ISO HO 0004	Named perils: coverage to a tenant for direct damage to personal property, personal liability and medical payments to others.
Comprehensive	ISO HO 0005	Named perils: Special + damage to other structures and personal property loss (most comprehensive coverage available for homeowners).
Unit Owners	ISO HO 0006	Named perils: causes of loss that are similar to the Homeowners 3 special causes of loss policy form.

Modified	ISO HO 0008	Named perils: damage to property, personal liability and medical payments to others for homes that are owner-occupied. Insurance limits are typically equal to the replacement cost of the home, where market value may be less than the replacement cost.

Dwelling (DP)

Coverage Form	ISO #	Perils Covered
Basic	ISO DP 0001	Named perils: damage to dwellings and personal property caused by named perils that include fire, lightning, and explosions (that are internal).
Broad	ISO DP 0002	Named perils: Basic + damage to other structures and personal property loss.
Special	ISO DP 0003	Open perils: dwellings and structures; Named perils: personal property on a broad coverage basis.

Inland marine insurance provides coverage for property that must meet the guidelines set forth by the **National Association of Insurance Commissioners Nationwide Marine** definition:

- Property must be in transit
- Property must be moveable
- Property must be related to transportation or communication, or
- Property must be in the possession of a bailee

Under the *National Marine definition*, the six types of property subject to coverage are:

1. Imports
2. Exports
3. Domestic shipments and property in transit for sale or consignment
4. Bridges, tunnels and communications towers (and other instruments transportation and communication)
5. Property not usually held at a residence
6. Property that is related to a business practice or profession

Common **floaters**, specific types of coverage forms associated with *inland marine insurance*, include:

- Accounts Receivable floater
- Builders risk floater
- Commercial articles floater (i.e. fine arts, photographic equipment, musical instruments, etc.)
- Contractor's equipment floater

- Computer systems floater
- Display sign floater
- Equipment dealers floater
- Installation floater
- Jewelry floater
- Valuable papers and records floater

Flood insurance covers direct damage to buildings and their content within a community that participated in the **National Flood Insurance Program** (NFIP). The NFIP is a federally funded program that was established in 1968, making funds available to communities impacted by flooding. Policies are issued by private insurers that are certified to participate in the program by NFIP. The program is administered by the Federal Emergency Management Agency (FEMA) of the U.S. Department of Homeland Security.

Key Definitions

TERM	DEFINITION
Bailees	An individual entrusted with servicing, storing or repairing property.
Builders risk coverage form	Coverage provided for loss resulting in direct damage to buildings under construction. Covered property under this form include buildings and structures, foundations, fixtures and machinery, equipment and materials and supply used in construction.
Building and personal property coverage form (BPP)	Coverage provided for loss resulting in direct damage to buildings, business personal property and personal property of others. The coverage form does not include coverage for liability.
Business auto coverage (BAP)	Coverage for loss due to damage and liability caused by a vehicle in use for business purposes. Coverage for auto related businesses (i.e. repair shops and trucking companies) are excluded.
Commercial general liability (CGL)	Covers claims of liability for bodily injury and property damage (Coverage Part A) related to the operations of a business, and personal and advertising injury (Coverage Part B).
Commercial package policy	Commercial property insurance coverage forms that combine

TERM	DEFINITION
(CPP)	different coverages under a single package.
Commercial property basic causes of loss (CP-1)	Coverage provided in a commercial and property policy for the following named covered perils: fire, lightning, explosion, smoke, and windstorm. Other perils that may be covered include loss due to hail, riot and civil commotion, aircraft, vehicles, vandalism, sprinkler leakage, sinkhole collapse, and volcanic action.
Commercial property broad causes of loss (CP-2)	Coverage provided in a commercial and property policy for the following named covered perils in addition to those listed in the basic causes of loss form: falling objects; weight of snow, ice, or sleet; water damage and collapse from a specified cause.
Commercial property causes of loss form	Forms that provide coverage for a specified cause of loss as stated in the form. There are three types of cause of loss forms: basic (CP-1), broad (CP-2) and special (CP-3).
Commercial property special causes of loss (CP-3)	Coverage provided in a commercial and property policy for all causes of loss except for those that are specifically excluded from coverage.
Crime	Coverage for a business against loss due to acts of fraud or acts of dishonesty.
Dwelling basic causes of loss (DP-1)	Coverage provided for damage to dwellings and personal property caused by named perils that include fire, lightning, and explosions that are internal. Other perils made by added by endorsement.
Dwelling broad causes of loss (DP-2)	Coverage provided for damage to dwellings and personal property that is in addition to the basic causes of loss form (DP-1).
Dwelling insurance	A type of homeowners insurance that provides additional coverage for causes of loss not covered in a standard homeowners insurance policy.
Dwelling special causes of	Coverage provided for dwellings and structures on an all risks

TERM	DEFINITION
loss (DP-3)	basis and personal property on a broad causes of loss basis.
Earthquake and volcanic eruption endorsement	Additional coverage added to a causes of loss form (i.e. basic, broad or special) for damage resulting from an earthquake or eruption of a volcano.
Equipment breakdown coverage	Coverage for loss caused by damage of a mechanical or electrical nature and loss of use of equipment. Also includes revenue lost and extra expenses associated with the loss of use of the covered equipment.
Floater	A name for Inland Marine insurance.
Homeowners basic causes of loss (HO-1)	Coverage provided for damage to property, personal liability and medical payments to others. Not widely available in most states.
Homeowners broad causes of loss (HO-2)	Coverage provided for direct damage, any private structure attached to the property (i.e. garage), personal property at or away from the home and any loss of use.
Homeowners comprehensive causes of loss (HO-5)	Coverage provided in addition to the special causes of loss form that is considered the broadest causes of loss coverage form for homeowners, including other structures and personal property.
Homeowners contents broad causes of loss (HO-4)	Coverage provided to a tenant for direct damage to personal property based on a broad named perils basis. The form provides both personal liability coverage and medical payments coverage.
Homeowners modified coverage causes of loss (HO-8)	Coverage provided for damage to property, personal liability and medical payments to others for dwellings that are owner-occupied. Insurance limits are typically equal to the replacement cost of the home, where market value may be less than the replacement cost. Used primarily with older homes or those built with substandard materials.
Homeowners special causes of loss (HO-3)	Coverage provided in addition to the broad causes of loss form for homeowners insurance plus additional coverage for personal liability and medical payments to others.

TERM	DEFINITION
Homeowners unit owners causes of loss (HO-6)	Coverage provided for those insured that own a condominium or interest of mutual benefit in a cooperative building. Provides the level of coverage for causes of loss that is similar to the Homeowners 3 special causes of loss policy form.
Inland marine coverage	Coverage provides insurance for items shipped via land transportation as well as various items of transportation such as roads and bridges and communication items such as television radio towers.
Personal and advertising injury liability coverage	Coverage for loss associated with injury caused by false arrest, malicious prosecution, wrongful eviction, slander, libel, violation of a person's rights to privacy, misuse of advertising, and copyright infringement.
Property insurance	Insurance protection that provides the insured with indemnification against loss due to damage to covered property, such as buildings, land and equipment.

Chapter Questions

1. The causes of loss form in a commercial and property policy that provides the broadest level of coverage is known as:
A. Broad
B. Special
C. Basic
D. General

2. What is the most common form of homeowners causes of loss form purchased?
A. HO-3
B. HO-5
C. HO-6
D. HO-8

3. A Commercial Package Policy (CPP) includes all of the following EXCEPT:
I. BPP
II. Declaration
III. BAP
IV. Crime

A. I and II
B. I, II, III
C. I, III, IV
D. I, II, III and IV

4. What are perils are listed in a property insurance policy?
A. Specific
B. Listed
C. Named
D. Written

5. Which homeowners coverage form is used by the owners of condominium units or cooperative buildings?
A. HO-2
B. HO-4
C. HO-6
D. HO-8

Answer Key

1. The correct answer is **B**. The special causes of loss coverage form (ISO CP 10 30) is also referred to as the all risks coverage form, covering all causes of loss except for those that are specifically excluded in the policy.

2. The correct answer is **A**. The special causes of loss coverage form (HO-3) is the most common type of homeowners insurance coverage purchased.

3. The correct answer is **D**. A Commercial Package Policy includes a common policy declaration and conditions section and may also include a combination of Buildings and Business Personal Property (BPP), Crime, Equipment Breakdown, Inland Marine, Commercial General Liability (CGL), Personal and Advertising Injury Liability and Business Auto (BAP) coverages.

4. The correct answer is **C**. Perils that are specifically listed in a property insurance policy are referred to as named perils.

5. The correct answer is **C**. The homeowners unit owners causes of loss (HO-6) provides coverage for loss by owners of condominium units or shares of mutual benefits in a cooperative building.

CASUALTY INSURANCE BASICS

Casualty insurance is also called **liability** insurance. Whereas property insurance provides protection against loss for physical assets such as land, buildings and goods, casualty insurance involves claims that involve a *third-party* (which is why it may also be referred to as **third-party insurance**). A property insurance claim takes place between two parties (insurer and insured), casualty insurance involves the *insured* as the **first party**, *insurer* as the **second party** and a **claimant** as the **third party** (Figure 6).

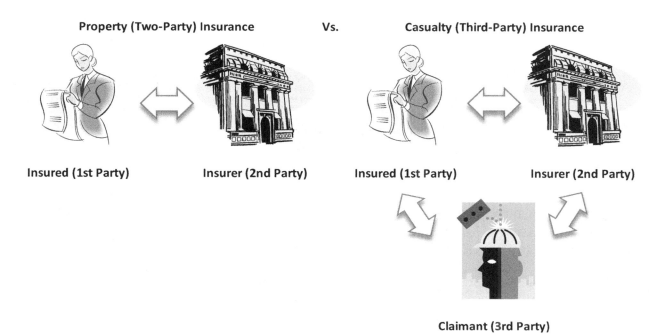

Property (Two-Party) Insurance   Vs.   **Casualty (Third-Party) Insurance**

Insured (1st Party)   **Insurer (2nd Party)**   **Insured (1st Party)**   **Insurer (2nd Party)**

Claimant (3rd Party)

Figure 6 2-Party vs. 3-Party Insurance

- In property insurance, the insured is the primary party to the policy. There exists a **named insured** to whom all of the rights and responsibilities are ascribed. The *named insured* appears in the *declaration page* of the policy. The first insured whose name appears in the declaration page is the first named insured. Subsequent insured customers are known as **additional insured** (which may be a person or entity covered by **endorsement**).
- In casualty insurance, the *claimant* comes into the policy when a loss occurs, resulting in injury or other damage to the third party.

Legal Liability of the 1st Party

Casualty (or liability) insurance involves the injury or damage by the *insured* (1st party) being inflicted on a *claimant* (3rd party). This is referred to as the legal liability of the 1st party to the 3rd party. This liability is determined when the insured is the *cause* of the injury or damage to a claimant (see Figure 7).

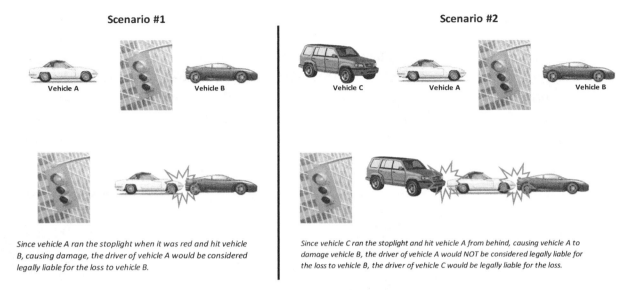

Scenario #1

Scenario #2

Since vehicle A ran the stoplight when it was red and hit vehicle B, causing damage, the driver of vehicle A would be considered legally liable for the loss to vehicle B.

Since vehicle C ran the stoplight and hit vehicle A from behind, causing vehicle A to damage vehicle B, the driver of vehicle A would NOT be considered legally liable for the loss to vehicle B, the driver of vehicle C would be legally liable for the loss.

Figure 7 Examples of legal liability

Tort

A **tort** is a legal term that refers to injurious harm inflicted by one party on another party. Under tort law, the party upon whom harm was caused may seek reasonable compensation from the party inflicting the harm. The nature of torts may be either civil (negligence) or criminal (deliberate) acts that are deemed wrongful.

> - **Unintentional** torts are acts caused by negligence on the part of one party toward another party. Negligence can be a failure to act or exercise the same level of reasonable care that another person in a similar situation would have exhibited.
> - **Intentional** torts are acts that are deliberate in nature. The law permits a party intentionally harmed by an intentional tort to seek legal redress.

In terms of liability insurance, acts that are negligent (*unintentional torts*) would be covered whereas deliberate acts (*intentional torts*) would not be.

Vicarious Liability

Vicarious liability extends liability to a person who is held responsible for the conduct of another person. One of the best examples of vicarious liability is that of a parent's responsibility for their child or children. Vicarious liability may also extend to an employer's responsibility for the acts of their employees (while on the job) and a business's responsibility for any independent contractors working on behalf of the company.

Absolute and Strict Liability

Absolute and **strict** liability holds that the insured as first party may be held legally liable for a loss suffered by the third party, even in the absence of negligence. Under *absolute liability*, the first party is deemed liable for injury or damages that occur because of activity that is or could be considered dangerous. This standard would apply to animal owners or producers of products deemed dangerous (or potentially dangerous). *Strict liability* is usually applied in cases of product liability cases, where the manufacturer produced a defective product (i.e. automobiles, window coverings that cause a choking hazard, etc.) or fail to warn the public of a potential risk (i.e. hot McDonald's coffee).

Damages

When a loss occurs involving a claimant against the insured, there are compensatory awards that may be provided to make up for the loss. These awards are known as damages; two types of damage awards are **compensatory (special** and **general)** and **punitive**.

- *Compensatory damages* are used to provide the claimant with a restoration of their value prior to the loss. Compensatory damages are comprised of two distinct types: *special damages* (which are for quantifiable or tangible losses that occur) and *general damages* (which account for intangibles such as pain and suffering associated with the loss).
- *Punitive damages* are awards made with designed purpose of punishing or discouraging certain types of behavior.

Type of Loss

A casualty insurance policy provided coverage for loss suffered by a third party (claimant). The types of loss covered are **bodily injury** and **property damage**.

- *Bodily injury* is any illness, sickness, disease or harm (including death) that results from the negligence of one party toward another party.
- *Property damage* is physical damage resulting in loss to the property owned by a third party.

A first party may be liable for a *bodily injury* sustained by a third party, for example, if the third party were to slip and fall on the sidewalk of the first party's home, resulting in a broken leg. The types of damages paid may include the cost of hospitalization, surgery, and any required durable medical equipment (*compensatory special damages*). The payment by the first party's insurance company under a casualty insurance policy to the third party may also include an agreed upon amount for pain and suffering (*compensatory general damages*).

Medical Payments to Others

In addition to covering losses resulting in damage to property or bodily injury, casualty insurance also provides a benefit in the form of **medical payments to others**. This form of coverage may be provided by the *insurer* (second party) to a *claimant* (third party), even if the *insured* (first party) is not *legally liable* for the *bodily injury* suffered by the claimant. The purpose of this protection is to prevent lawsuits emanating from liability claims.

Most policies allow a claimant a period of up to 2 years after an accident resulting in bodily injury occurred to file a claim. The payment provides for expenses deemed medically necessary by the insurer.

Personal Liability Insurance

When a claimant suffers financial harm as a result of the negligence of the insured, that is neither due to bodily injury or property damage, this type of claim is addressed with **personal liability insurance**. Coverage for personal liability may be provided as an *endorsement* to the policy (an additional level of coverage added to the policy) or as a stand-alone policy. Types of actions that may result in personal liability include libel, slander, infringement of a copyright and false imprisonment.

Accidents and Occurrences

The types of events that are the cause of loss in casualty insurance coverage can be classified as either **accidents** or **occurrences**.

- *Accidents* are events that are unforeseen, unintentional and unexpected that result in damage or a loss to occur.
- *Occurrences* include accidents or exposure to certain conditions on an ongoing or continuous basis (i.e. exposure to asbestos) that results in bodily injury or property damage to a third party.

Concept Review

Casualty insurance is also known as **liability insurance**. It provides coverage for loss due to injury or damages suffered by a **third party** (**claimant**) resulting from the actions of a **first party** (*insured*). The *insurer* is referred to as the **second party** in a casualty insurance relationship. This differs from *property insurance* where loss or damages suffered by a **named insured** (as listed in the **declaration page** of the policy) constitute a trigger of benefits paid by the insurer to the insured (a **two party** relationship); any **additional insured customers** to a property insurance policy may be included by **endorsement** to the policy but rights are subordinate to the *named insured*.

When the insured is deemed **legally liable** for the cause of the loss to the claimant, the insurer will pay the amount of loss as a benefit to the third party. The cause of loss is based on a **tort**, a legal term for injurious harm inflicted by one party onto another party. Torts, which are civil and criminal, may be **unintentional** acts caused by negligence (for which casualty insurance covers) and **intentional** acts, which are deliberate in nature and are not covered by insurance. The conduct of another person under control or responsibility of a first party that causes a loss for a third party results in **vicarious liability** for the first party. Such control/responsibility relationships include employers and employees and parents and children. Even if negligence is not present, a first party may still deemed liable for loss that causes **bodily injury** (sickness, illness, disease or harm including death) or **property damage** (physical damage to property owned by a third party). **Absolute liability** deems the insured liable because of activity engaged in that is deemed dangerous. **Strict liability** (mostly applied to product liability cases) addresses defective products or the insured's failure to warn the public about a known or potential risk.

When loss occurs resulting in a claim by a third party against a first party, a damage award is made to compensate the claimant for the value of their loss. The main types of damage awards include **compensatory** (**special** and **general**) and **punitive** damages. *Compensatory damages* provide a restoration to previous value prior to the loss. A *special damage* award is based on a quantitative and tangible loss while *general damage* awards take into account intangible costs, such as pain and suffering. *Punitive damages* are awarded to punish negligent behavior or as a deterrent against certain types of behavior.

In addition to providing for loss resulting in *bodily injury* and/or *property damage*, casualty insurance may also make **medical payments to others** who are impacted by the loss. The purpose of this form of coverage is to discourage lawsuits or liability claims from occurring as a result of the loss, covering those expenses deemed medically necessary. A claimant may file a claim with the insurer for a period up to 2 years after the accident occurred.

A claimant who suffers a loss that is attributed to a cause that is not bodily injury or property damage, such a claim is addressed with **personal liability insurance**. *Personal liability insurance*, which can be a stand-alone policy or an **endorsement** to a policy, covers such actions like libel, slander, copyright infringement and false imprisonment.

Accidents and **occurrences** are types of events that cause a loss. An *accident* is an event that is unintentional, unexpected and unforeseen resulting in a loss or damage to occur. An *occurrence*, which includes accidents, are an ongoing or constant exposure to conditions that result in *bodily injury* or *property damage*.

Key Definitions

TERM	DEFINITION
Absolute liability	Standard of liability in the absence of negligence that holds a first party responsible for loss experienced by a third party due to the dangerous nature of an activity.
Bodily injury	Loss coverage provided for injury, illness, sickness, and harm (including death) suffered by a third party as a result of the negligence of a first party.
Claimant	The third party in casualty insurance to whom injury or loss occurs.
Compensatory damages	A type of damage awarded to a claimant designed to restore them to their pre-loss value.
Endorsement	An additional level of coverage attached to an issued policy of insurance.
First party	The insured.
General damages	A damage award paid for intangible loss (i.e. pain and suffering).
Intentional tort	Injury or harm caused as the result of acts that are deliberate in nature.
Legal Liability	The standard used to determine the party responsible for a loss (cause).
Personal liability insurance	A type of coverage for loss due to the negligence of the insured that is neither based on a bodily injury or property damage.
Property damage	Loss coverage for physical damage to property owned by a third party caused by the negligence of a first party.
Punitive damages	A type of damage award designed to punish and/or

TERM	DEFINITION
	discourage behavior.
Second party	The insurer.
Special damages	A damage award paid for tangible loss.
Strict liability	See absolute liability. Typically applied in product liability cases.
Third party	The claimant.
Third-party insurance	A term used to define casualty insurance.
Tort	Injurious harm caused by one party on another.
Unintentional tort	Injury or harm caused as the result of acts that are the result of negligence.
Vicarious liability	Legal liability extended to a person who is responsible for the actions of another person.

Chapter Questions

1. With casualty insurance, the parties to the policy when a claim is made are:
   I.   Insured
   II. Insurer
   III. Claimant

   A. I and II
   B. II and III
   C. I, II and III
   D. I and III

2. Casualty insurance provides coverage for acts that are:
   A. Intentional
   B. Unintentional
   C. Negligent
   D. B and C only

3. A third party claim under coverage for medical payments to others must occur within what period of time?
   A. 6 months after the accident occurred
   B. 1 year after the accident occurred
   C. 2 years after the accident occurred
   D. Immediately after the accident occurred

4. What type of liability standard applies to product liability cases?
   A. Strict
   B. Absolute
   C. Vicarious
   D. Legal

5. Accidents are events that occur, which are:
   I.   Unforeseen
   II. Intentional
   III. Unexpected

   A. I only
   B. I and III
   C. I and II
   D. I, II and III

Answer Key

1. The correct answer is **C**. Casualty insurance, which is also referred to as third party insurance, involves three parties in a claim, the insured as the first party, the insurer as the second party and the claimant as the third party to the claim.

2. The correct answer is **D**. Casualty insurance provides coverage for acts committed by one party against another party that are unintentional in nature or the result of negligence. A deliberate or intentional act would not be covered by casualty or any form of insurance.

3. The correct answer is **C**. Under the medical payments to others coverage, a third party claim for bodily injury must occur within 2 years of the accident.

4. The correct answer is **A**. Strict liability, which is the standard typically applied to product liability cases, is the failure of a manufacturer to recall a defective product or provide label warnings, resulting in loss due to injury or damage to a third party in the absence of negligence on the part of the manufacturer.

5. The correct answer is **B**. An accident is an event that is unforeseen, unintentional and unexpected. An event that is intentional for the purpose of creating a loss would be deemed a deliberate act and not be insurable.

TYPES OF CASUALTY INSURANCE

Casualty insurance is also referred to as *liability* insurance. Casualty insurance deals with loss due to *personal injury*, damage to property of others and legal liability. Refer to the previous chapter for information on basic principles in connection with *casualty insurance* coverage. Types of casualty insurance coverage include **automotive** insurance, **commercial crime** insurance, **commercial general liability** (CGL) insurance and **Workers' Compensation** insurance.

Automotive Insurance (Commercial and Personal)

Automotive insurance provides protection for commercial and personal vehicles that are involved in loss that cause *bodily injury* or damage to property.

Commercial Auto Coverage

Commercial auto coverage includes these coverage forms:

- **Business auto** coverage form that provides liability coverage for any vehicle owned, leased, borrowed or hired by the business.
- **Garage** coverage form protects a business that is involved in the repair, service, sales, storage or parking of a vehicle.
- **Truckers** coverage form, which is used mainly by common carriers; most transportation companies use the *motor carrier* coverage form.
- **Business auto physical damage** coverage form that provides coverage for collision, comprehensive, towing, glass breakage and extensions for special coverage.

Multiple coverage forms may be used in one commercial auto coverage policy.

Personal Auto Coverage

Personal auto coverage protects individual vehicle owners form bodily injury and physical damage as well as medical payments to others and liability arising from loss related to a vehicle accident, theft or other damage to the car. Coverage for *personal auto* insurance must be for a vehicle that is an owned private passenger type and not used for business purposes.

A *personal auto* insurance policy is comprised of six parts:

- **Part A**, Liability coverage
- **Part B**, Medical payments coverage
- **Part C**, Uninsured motorists coverage
- **Part D**, Coverage for damage to the insured's auto
- **Part E**, Duties after an accident or loss
- **Part F**, General coverage provisions

There are also **supplementary parts** that may be included as part of a *personal auto* insurance policy, which are also referred to as **special endorsements**.

Commercial Crime Insurance

Commercial crime insurance policies (also referred to as **fidelity insurance**) protect businesses against loss from acts of dishonesty or fraud. These incidents include employee theft, robbery, burglary, loss of money, securities and property. Other types of loss covered by a commercial crime policy include embezzlement, forgery, computer fraud, wire fraud and acts of employee dishonesty.

Crime, as defined in a crime insurance policy, includes:

- **Theft**, which is property that has been unlawfully taken.
- **Burglary** is theft of property from a business premises, safe or vault owned by the business that involves trespassing and signs of forced entry or exit.
- **Robbery**, which is similar to burglary except it involves an individual and must involve force or threat of violence.
- **Disappearance** of property not involving theft, burglary or robbery.

Commercial Crime Coverage Forms

Commercial crime coverage insurance is issued under two coverage forms: **loss-sustained form** and **discovery form**. The *loss-sustained form* is similar to the *occurrence form* for a *commercial general liability* (CGL) policy (see below section) and the discovery form is similar to the CGL *claims-made form*. Commercial entities that are private enterprises use the **Commercial Crime Coverage Form**; entities that are government employers use the **Government Crime Coverage Form**.

Types of Commercial Crime Coverages

There are eight types of coverage that an insured may select for a crime coverage form.

- Theft
- Forgery
- Theft of money or securities (inside the premises)
- Robbery or burglary (inside the premises)
- Theft, robbery or burglary outside the premises
- Computer fraud
- Funds transfer fraud
- Money orders and counterfeiting

Commercial General Liability Insurance

As discussed in the chapter entitled *Types of Property Insurance* under *commercial package policy* optional parts, **commercial general liability** (CGL) insurance protects businesses from liability associated with bodily injury and property damage associated with the property of the business, operations, products, completed operations and advertising and personal injury liability. These are known as the **liability exposures** to a business that make the business vulnerable to loss. This type of protection, which has been in existence since 1986, replaces its prior coverage form, comprehensive general liability insurance.

- **Premises and operations** liability exposure deals with the legal liability of a business for loss that occurs arising from its premises (physical property) and operations. A covered occurrence must occur within the coverage territory specified in the policy during the policy period.
- **Products** liability exposure relates to goods and merchandise of the business that is manufactured, sold, handled, distributed or disposed of by the business (either by the insured or any person under the direction of the business, such as employees and contractors).
- **Completed operations** liability exposure is in connection to finished services provided to customers, product installation, construction and repairs performed. Liability for completed operations starts once the work performed by the insured is completed and the insured has left the worksite.
- **Contingent liability** exposure deals with a business's liability for the actions of others while under its direction or control. This includes contractors and others who have a contractual relationship with the business to perform work. The relationship between the business and the contractor may be as outlines in a service contract to perform work, hold harmless or indemnification agreement or lease agreement.

CGL Coverage Forms

Commercial general liability insurance is issued under two coverage forms: an **occurrence form** and **claims-made form**. The language provided in either form is identical; the differences between an *occurrence form* and a *claims-made form* has to do with when coverage is active, known as the **coverage trigger**. Under the *occurrence form*, the *coverage trigger* is when the *occurrence* (continuous or repeated exposure to loss) takes place during the policy period. The loss may be reported during the policy period or after. For the *claims-made form*, the *coverage trigger* takes place when the *occurrence* takes place after the policy's retroactive period and is reported during the policy period. All *occurrences* for either form must take place within the policy's coverage territory.

CGL Policy Sections

The policy sections of the commercial general liability coverage include:

- **Coverage A** provides for liability related to bodily injury and property damage.
- **Coverage B** provides for liability related personal and advertising injury.
- **Coverage C** provides for liability related to medical payments to others.
- **Supplementary payments** provide supplemental payments in additional to coverage liabilities for Coverage A and B.

Workers' Compensation Insurance

Workers' compensation insurance, established by the National Council on Compensation Insurance (NCCI), pays for work-related injuries to employees. Non-work related injuries are not covered by workers' compensation. An act of negligence on the behalf of the employer is deemed presumptuous in establishing liability for the employee's injury, although payments are made regardless of employer or the employee's negligence. Workers' compensation is mandated by the states whose laws vary.

States determine the nature of *workers' compensation* coverage, whether it is required or **compulsory** of employers or an **elective** to an employer doing business in the state. Laws governing *workers' compensation* may require the employer to pay in to a fund managed by the state (**monopolistic** laws) or from a private insurer on a **competitive** basis. Workers considered exempt from workers' compensation include:

- Agricultural workers
- Domestic workers
- Officers and directors of corporations
- Sole proprietors and self-employed individuals

In most states, a person's immigration status is excluded from consideration of eligibility for *workers' compensation*.

Injury is deemed to be any sickness, illness, disability or death that is related to *injury* loss caused by an accident or occurrence that is on the job (employment related) Benefits provided to an injured worker by *workers' compensation* include:

- Lost wages or income
- Medical payments
- Rehabilitation
- Survivorship benefits (if the result of an employment related injury is death).

Concept Review

Casualty insurance is also referred to as liability insurance, which provides protection for loss that arises from personal injury, property damage and legal liability of the insured. Coverage types include **automobile** insurance (commercial and personal), **commercial crime** insurance, **commercial general liability** (CGL) insurance and **workers' compensation** insurance.

Automobile insurance provides protection for bodily injury, property damage and medical payments to others for loss caused by the use of a vehicle, damage or theft of the vehicle. Commercial auto insurance coverage forms include:

- **Business auto** coverage form
- **Garage** coverage form
- **Truckers / Motor carrier** coverage form
- **Business auto physical damage** coverage form

Personal auto insurance is comprised of six policy parts:

- **Part A**, Liability coverage
- **Part B**, Medical payments coverage
- **Part C**, Uninsured motorists coverage
- **Part D**, Coverage for damage to the insured's auto
- **Part E**, Duties after an accident or loss
- **Part F**, General coverage provisions

Additionally, there are **supplementary parts** referred to as **special endorsements** to the personal auto insurance policy.

Commercial crime insurance (also known as **fidelity insurance**) provides protection to a business for acts of theft, fraud and dishonesty. The types of incidents include theft, burglary, robbery, loss of money and securities, as well as computer-related fraud, forgery and embezzlement. *Commercial crime* policies define crime as **theft** (unlawfully taking of property), **burglary** (theft of property from premises), **robbery** (theft of property from an individual) and **disappearance** (not involving theft, burglary or robbery). Commercial crime policies may be issued with one of two coverage types: **loss-sustained form** and **discovery form**. The *loss-sustained form* is similar to the CGL **occurrence form**; the *discovery form* is similar to the CGL **claims-made form**. Commercial entities use the **Commercial Crimes Coverage Form** and government employers use the **Government Crime Coverage Form**. Types of crimes covered include:

- Theft
- Forgery
- Theft of money or securities (inside the premises)
- Robbery or burglary (inside the premises)
- Theft, robbery or burglary outside the premises
- Computer fraud

- Funds transfer fraud
- Money orders and counterfeiting

Commercial general liability (CGL) coverage protects a business from liability that arises from bodily injury and property damage from a business and its premise and operations, products, completed operations and advertising and personal injury liability. A business's vulnerability to loss is referred to as its **liability exposure**. The coverage forms available for *commercial general liability* coverage include the *occurrence form* that is active (**coverage trigger**) when the *occurrence* happens during the policy period, or the *claims-made form* that is active when an *occurrence* happens during the **retroactive period** and is reported during the *policy period*.

The policy sections of CGL coverage include:

- **Coverage A** provides for liability related to bodily injury and property damage.
- **Coverage B** provides for liability related personal and advertising injury.
- **Coverage C** provides for liability related to medical payments to others.
- **Supplementary payments** provides supplemental payments in additional to coverage liabilities for Coverage A and B.

Workers' Compensation insurance pays for injuries to an employee that occur on the job or in an employment-related activity. Non-work related injuries to an employee are not covered under *workers' compensation* coverage. Workers' compensation, which is state-mandated, is required on a **compulsory** (required) or **elective** basis depending on the laws of the state. Employers who pay into a state-run fund for benefits are subject to a **monopolistic** system while employers in states that free to purchase coverage from any private insurer participate in a **competitive** *worker's compensation* system. Workers who are exempt from workers' compensation include domestic help, agricultural employees, corporate officers and directors and individuals who are sole proprietors or self-employed. An individual's immigration status may not be used as a basis for determining eligibility for workers' compensation in most states. Benefits payable under workers' compensation based on employment related **injury** (any sickness, illness, disability and death) include:

- Lost wages or income;
- Medical payments;
- Rehabilitation; and
- Survivorship benefits (if the result of an employment related injury is death).

Key Definitions

TERM	DEFINITION
Auto insurance	Protection for loss related to bodily injury and property

TERM	DEFINITION
	damage caused by a vehicle under the control or operation of the insured.
Casualty insurance	Protection for loss related to personal liability, property damage and legal liability.
Claims-made form	CGL coverage form that pays claims for occurrences that take place after the retroactive period and are reported during the policy period.
Commercial crime	Protection for loss due to acts of fraud, theft and dishonesty.
Commercial general liability (CGL)	Protection for loss due to bodily injury and property damage for a business related to liability from its premise and operations, products, completed operations and any personal and advertising injury.
Completed operations liability exposure	Loss arising from finished services provided, installation, construction and repairs performed after the insured has left a worksite.
Contingent liability exposure	Loss arising from a business's liability for the actions of others under their control or direction.
Coverage A	Covers bodily injury and property damage liability in a CGL.
Coverage B	Covers personal and advertising injury liability in a CGL.
Coverage C	Covers medical payments to others in a CGL.
Coverage trigger	The point under a CGL coverage form where coverage is activated.
Injury	Any sickness, illness and death that occurs related to an employee's employment related activities.
Liability exposures	Known liability (perils) that make a business vulnerable to loss. These include: (1) premises and operations; (2) products; (3) completed operations; and, (4) contingent liability.
Occurrence form	CGL coverage form that pays claims for occurrences that take

TERM	DEFINITION
	place during the policy period.
Premises and operations liability exposure	Loss arising from the physical premises or operations of the business.
Products liability exposure	Loss arising from liability associated with goods and merchandise manufactured, sold, handled, distributed and disposed of by the business.
Supplementary payments	Provides supplemental payments under Coverages A and B.
Workers' Compensation insurance	Protection for loss due to employee injury from an employment related activity.

Chapter Questions

1. A coverage trigger that happens when an occurrence takes place during the retroactive period and is reported during the policy period describes what type of commercial general liability form?
   A. Occurrence
   B. Claims-made
   C. Both A and B
   D. Neither A or B

2. Which policy section of a commercial general liability policy provide for liability arising from medical payments to others?
   A. Coverage A
   B. Coverage B
   C. Coverage C
   D. Supplementary payments

3. Workers' Compensation benefits paid are determined by what entity?
   A. NAIC
   B. State government
   C. Federal government
   D. NCCI

4. Each of the following is considered exempt from workers' compensation, EXCEPT:
   A. Agricultural workers
   B. Domestic workers
   C. Sole proprietors
   D. Illegal immigrants

5. Which of the following are considered crimes under a commercial crime insurance policy?
   A. Theft
   B. Burglary
   C. Robbery
   D. All of the following are considered crimes

Answer Key

1. The correct answer is **B**. The coverage trigger in a claims-made form for commercial general liability coverage takes place when an occurrence occurs in a retroactive period and is reported during the policy period.

2. The correct answer is **C**. Coverage C provides for liability arising from medical payments made to others.

3. The correct answer is **B**. Workers' compensation benefits payable to an employee injured due to a work related accident or occurrence are determined by the state in which the accident or occurrence took place.

4. The correct answer is **D**. Agricultural and domestic workers, along with sole proprietors are examples of workers that may be exempt from a state's workers' compensation requirements. Immigration status is typically excluded as a reason to deny workers' compensation coverage to an employee (in most states).

5. The correct answer is **D**. Choices A, B and C are all defined as crimes under a commercial crime insurance policy.

OTHER TYPES OF POLICIES

The different additional types of commercial lines of insurance that are available include: aviation, farm property, motor truck cargo, ocean marine and umbrella and excess liability insurance coverages, as well as surety and fidelity bonds.

Aviation Insurance

Aviation insurance provides protection related to the aircraft (**aircraft hull coverage**) and the

operations of the aircraft or airport (**airport liability coverage**). *Aviation insurance* is a highly specialized area of risk handled by a limited number of insurers with expertise in the aviation industry.

Aircraft hull coverage provides protection to the owner of an aircraft (*insured*) against loss due to damage. Coverage may be provided as an endorsement to *commercial general liability* coverage or as a separate policy (where coverage is excluded in a *named perils* CGL).

Aircraft liability coverage provides protection for passengers and other claimants (*third party*) who experience loss from *physical damage* or *bodily injury* caused by the use of an airport's premises.

Farm Property Insurance

Farm property insurance (also referred to as *farmowners* or *farm insurance*) provides coverage to meet the needs of a farmer. Coverage provided under a farm property insurance policy include *homeowners* (where the farmer's residence is located on the farm property), *commercial property* coverage and *commercial liability* coverage. The coverage provided by a *farm property insurance* policy meets the unique needs of farmers to protect their property interests as homeowners as well as business interests as farm owners (ranchers may also be covered by a *farm property* policy).

Fidelity Bonds

A **fidelity bond** is a type of insurance coverage that protects an employer against acts of theft. This includes the theft of money, securities and property owned or controlled by the employer. This type of coverage is written on a per loss basis and may be included as part of a *commercial crime* policy. It may also be referred to as **employee dishonesty coverage**.

Motor Truck Cargo Insurance

Motor truck cargo insurance (a form of inland marine insurance, as discussed in the chapter entitled *Types of Property Insurance*) covers loss arising from damage or missing property in transit. Such transit loss may take place via a common carrier or the use of the insured's own vehicle based on the coverage form used.

Ocean Marine Insurance

Ocean marine insurance provides coverage for the transportation of goods and merchandise via waters that may be either domestic (U.S.) or international. *Ocean marine* also includes inland marine and aviation transit coverage forms that are connected to the ocean transport of the goods and merchandise. *Ocean marine insurance* evolved from early forms rooted in ancient Greek and Roman cultures with its modern form being codified in England in the 1600s, making it the oldest form of any insurance protection.

There are four forms of coverage for ocean marine insurance: (1) hull or ocean vessel; (2) cargo; (3) freight revenue; and, (4) legal liability.

- **Hull** coverage provides protection to the owner of an ocean transport vessel that experiences a loss caused by damage to the vessel.
- **Cargo** coverage protects loss due to damage to any cargo contained on an ocean transport vessel.
- **Freight revenue** coverage protects the revenues owed the owner of the ocean transport vessel due to loss caused by damaged or destroyed cargo.
- **Liability** coverage is similar to liability coverage provided in commercial general liability coverage.

Loss settlement for ocean marine insurance is based on the amount or percentage stated in the **coinsurance clause**. A policy containing a 100 percent *coinsurance clause* will pay for the total value of loss; a *coinsurance clause* of 50 percent means that the insurer will pay for a partial loss of up to 50 percent of the value of the loss. Additionally, *ocean marine* policies contain warranties (as discussed in the chapter entitled *Insurance Basics*). The payment for loss is contingent on meeting the requirements of the warranty (a breach of the warranty will result in no payment). The two types of warranties in an ocean marine insurance policy are:

- **Expressed warranties** are written into the policy and may include exclusions for war, riots and acts of civil commotion.
- **Implied warranties** are not written in the policy but are generally acceptable prohibitions such as sea-worthiness of the vessel and the qualifications of the vessel's captain and crew.

Surety Bonds

A **surety bond** (unlike a *fidelity bond*) is a form of *third party* insurance whereby the *first party* (**surety**) guarantees the performance of a *second party* (*principal*) to a *third party* (**obligee**). A common example of a surety bond would be that of a construction company who takes out a construction bond guaranteeing the work of contractors for the completion of work by a certain time to the building's owner.

Umbrella and Excess Liability Insurance

Umbrella and excess liability insurance is a type of coverage that protects the insured from any liability that may arise in excess of their existing coverage. This type of coverage typically provides protection in the event of catastrophic loss and may be available in both commercial and personal lines of protection.

An *umbrella and excess liability coverage* is issued in connection with existing coverage for the specified loss. The existing coverage is referred to as the **primary insurance**. For example, umbrella and excess liability coverage for a general liability would be issued as an umbrella for a business's underlying *commercial general liability, commercial auto* and *employer liability* coverages. Because *umbrella and excess liability* insurance is based on the policy limits and other provisions of the underlying primary insurance(s), there is no standard policy form.

Concept Review

Additional commercial lines of insurance **aviation insurance**, **farm property insurance**, **motor truck cargo insurance**, **ocean marine insurance**, **umbrella and excess liability insurance** and **fidelity** and **surety bonds**.

Aviation insurance provides coverage for owners of aircrafts against loss caused by damage to an airplane (**aviation hull coverage**) and protection against loss for claimants due to bodily injury and property damage at an airport or due to the airport's operation (**airport liability coverage**). *Farm property insurance* covers the home of a farmer or rancher (homeowners), the *commercial property* of the farmer and any commercial or personal liability arising from the farm or ranch operation or the farmer's residence (*commercial liability coverage*).

A form of *inland marine coverage, motor truck cargo insurance* provides coverage for loss arising from damage or the loss of property in inland transit. *Ocean marine insurance* provides protection for the transportation of goods and merchandise via domestic or international waterways. The earliest recorded form of insurance protection, there are four basic types of ocean marine coverage forms: (1) **hull/vessel coverage**; (2) **cargo coverage**; (3) **freight revenue coverage**; and, (4) **legal liability coverage**. The **loss settlement** for ocean marine coverage is based on a percentage stated in the **coinsurance clause**. A clause of 50 percent pays an amount associated with a partial loss for the associated coverage form. The basis for the payment of the *coinsurance amount* is based on a warranty that is either written in the policy (**expressed warranties**) or generally accepted (**implied warranties**), such as the sea-worthiness of the ocean transport vessel.

Umbrella and excess liability insurance provides protection in excess of the loss limits for existing coverage (known as **primary insurance**). This protection typically covers loss that is of a catastrophic nature, which is a large loss that exceeds the stated limit of the primary insurance, such as a class action settlement or other tort action against the insured.

Employers looking for coverage against acts of theft committed by their employees (i.e. theft of money, securities and property owned or controlled by the employer) would purchase a *fidelity bond*. A *first party* (**surety**) guaranteeing the performance of a *second party* (*principal*) to a third party (*obligee*) does so with a *surety bond*.

Key Definitions

TERM	DEFINITION
Airport liability coverage	Protection for loss associated with bodily injury and property damage associated with the operations of an airport.
Aviation hull coverage	Protection for loss associated with damage to an airplane.
Aviation insurance	Protection for loss associated with property damage or bodily injury connected with airplanes and airports.
Cargo coverage	Protection for loss associated with cargo transported by an ocean transport vessel.
Coinsurance clause	The percentage amount paid for total or partial loss in ocean marine insurance coverage.
Expressed warranties	A warranty that is stated in ocean marine coverage.
Farm property insurance	Multiple forms of coverage for farmers (and ranchers) that provide protection for the home (homeowners), liability (commercial liability) and property (commercial property).
Fidelity bonds	Protection for loss associated with employee theft.
Freight revenue coverage	Protection for loss of revenue associated with freight loss or damaged during ocean transport.
Hull or vessel coverage	Protection for loss associated with damage to an ocean transport vessel or ship.
Implied warranties	A warranty that is generally accepted but not stated in ocean marine coverage.
Loss settlement	The settlement amount paid by ocean marine insurance.
Motor truck cargo insurance	A form of inland marine insurance that covers loss associated with damage or loss to cargo in transport.
Obligee	The party to whom the surety in a surety bond guarantees the performance of the principal.

TERM	DEFINITION
Ocean marine insurance	Protection for loss associated with damage to an ocean transport vessels hull, cargo, freight revenue or legal liability. Also includes aviation and inland marine coverage associated with waterway transportation.
Primary insurance	The underlying insurance in an umbrella and excess liability insurance policy.
Surety	The party who guarantees the performance of the principal to the obligee in a surety bond.
Surety bonds	Protection involving a first party (surety) guaranteeing the performance of a second party (principal) to a third party (obligee).
Umbrella and excess liability insurance	Provides protection in excess of the coverage provided by existing coverage (primary insurance) and may be wrapped with multiple related policies (i.e. commercial general liability, commercial auto, employer liability).

Chapter Questions

1. A surety bond is considered what type of insurance protection?
A. Fidelity
B. Third party
C. Two party
D. Property insurance

2. Ocean marine insurance provides for each of the following coverage forms, EXCEPT:
I. Hull
II. Airport
III. Liability

A. I only
B. I and II
C. I, II, and III
D. I and III

3. Which of the following warranties are included in an ocean marine insurance policy?
A. Expressed
B. Named
C. Implied
D. A and C only

4. What is the name of coverage that precedes an umbrella and excess liability insurance policy?
A. Excess
B. Stated
C. Primary
D. Secondary

5. All of the following are covered in a farm property insurance policy, EXCEPT:
A. Home
B. Barn
C. Corn crop
D. Personal liability

Answer Key

1. The correct answer is **B**. A surety bond is a form of third party coverage where a surety (first party) guarantees the performance of a principal (second party) to the third party (obligee).

2. The correct answer is **D**. The four ocean marine insurance coverage forms include: hull and vessel coverage; cargo coverage; freight revenue coverage; and, legal liability.

3. The correct answer is **D**. The types of warranties associated with an ocean marine insurance policy is expressed (written in the policy) and implied (not written but generally understood).

4. The correct answer is **C**. The coverage that proceeds coverage provided in an umbrella and excess liability policy is called primary insurance.

5. The correct answer is **C**. Farm crops are not covered under a farm property insurance policy; crops would be covered under crop insurance.

INSURANCE REGULATION

This section is a survey of the rules, laws and regulations that govern the practice of insurance agents and brokers, companies and other in the business of *risk transfer* on behalf of the insured. This is a general discussion and not specific to any particular state's laws or regulations.

Errors and Omissions

As discussed in the chapter entitled *Types of Casualty Insurance*, **Errors and Omissions** (E&O) coverage is a form of professional liability insurance that provides for loss due to negligence. E&O is typically provided to individuals and companies that are engaged in certain professions such as insurance, banking, accounting and legal.

The most common types of E&O claims filed against insurance agents include those that are based on **inadequacy** (obtaining the incorrect or improper coverage for the insured) and *negligence* (failing to provide relevant information concerning coverage and coverage benefits).

Federal Regulations

The following federal regulation affects insurance contracts and the practice of insurance agents and providers:

- **Fair Credit Reporting Act of 1971** (15 U.S.C. § 1681 et seq.) provides privacy protection to an insured. Under the provisions of the FCRA an applicant for insurance has a right to request any credit and other reporting data used in the determination to issue or deny coverage.

In addition to the FCRA, there are various federal laws that deal with insurance on a federal basis:

- **McCarran-Ferguson Act of 1945** (15 U.S.C.A. § 1011 et seq.) provides states with the ability to regulate the business of insurance, unless otherwise preempted by federal law. The law overturned the U.S. Supreme Court's ruling in *United States v. Southeastern Underwriters, 322 U.S. 533 (1944)*, which attempted to bring the regulation of insurance under the Commerce Clause of the U.S. Constitution.
- **Gramm-Leach-Bliley Financial Modernization Act of 1999** (15 U.S.C. § 80b-10a) removed the prohibition created by the *Glass-Steagall Act of 1933 (12 U.S.C. et seq.)* allowing banks, securities and insurance companies to engage in commercial and investment banking activities. The Act also set minimum standards for state insurance laws and regulations in order to prevent federal preemption.
- **Dodd-Frank Wall Street Reform and Consumer Protection Act of 2010** (15 U.S.C. § 78) created the **Consumer Financial Protection Bureau** (CFPB) as a federal oversight board for consumers in banking, securities and insurance.

National Association of Insurance Commissioners

Insurance, unlike securities and banking, is not regulated by a national agency. Insurance laws and regulations come from the state in which the insurer is located or doing business as either a *domestic*, *foreign* or *alien* insurer, making insurance a state based regulatory system.

The **National Association of Insurance Commissioners** (NAIC) is a standard setting organization in support of insurers, consumers and the insurance industry. The mission of the organization is to:

- Protect the public interest
- Promote competitive markets
- Facilitate the fair and equitable treatment of insurance consumers
- Promote the reliability, solvency and financial solidity of insurance and institutions
- Support and improve state regulation of insurance

NAIC is supported by the insurance commissioners from each of the 50 states as well as the District of Columbia, and the territories of American Samoa, Guam, Northern Mariana Islands, Puerto Rico, and the U.S. Virgin Islands. Model regulations and rules that are considered by the legislatures of NAIC's member commissions are created by the organization. NAIC has no federal oversight or regulatory authority over individual insurers, agents or brokers.

State Regulations

Insurance is regulated at the state level. Insurance law, which was first created in New Hampshire in 1851, was deemed outside the Commerce Clause (Article 1, Section 8, U.S. Constitution) under the ruling of *Paul v. Virginia, 75 U.S. 168* (1869). Although states are free to set their own laws with respect to the regulation of insurer providers and their representatives, many states subscribe to the model regulations recommended by NAIC.

Several model insurance regulations that have been adopted by the states include:

- **NAIC's Risk-Based Capital for Insurers Model Act** is a model act that applies to property and casualty insurers, as well as to life insurance companies. The act sets minimum capital levels that need to be maintained by an insurer in relationship to their amount of risk and allows state insurance regulators to take action against an insurer when risk capital thresholds are below required minimums.
- **Model Financial Regulation Standards and Accreditation Program** provides standards for states to accredit insurers based on their maintenance of a system of financial solvency.

Doctrine of Comity / Comity of States

The **doctrine of comity** or **comity of states** is the deference of one state's laws to the laws of another. This doctrine helps determine the governing jurisdiction, as in the case of group insurance or workers compensation, of a cause of action brought by a claimant against an insured.

Buyer's Guide to Insurance

A **Buyer's Guide to Insurance** provides insurance consumers with basic "need-to-know" information about insurance, as well as information for contacting a state's insurance commission for information or assistance. Many states require insurers to provide consumers with "*A Consumer's/Buyer's Guide to Auto/Car Insurance*" and "*A Consumer's/Buyer's Guide to Homeowners Insurance.*"

State Insurance Guaranty Association

The **state insurance guaranty association** protects policyholders and beneficiaries in circumstances where an insurer becomes insolvent or is unable to meet its claim paying obligations. Insurers doing business in each of the 50 states, Puerto Rico and the District of Columbia are required to be members of the respective state's insurance guaranty association. Generally there are two types of *state insurance guaranty associations* (SIGA), a life and health insurance SIGA and property and casualty insurance SIGA.

When a member insurer becomes insolvent or fails to meet its obligations, an assessment is made post-solvency of remaining member insurers based on their premium share. It is illegal under state law for an *insurance agent* or *broker* to mention the existence of SIGA as a benefit for policyholders or beneficiaries.

Concept Review

Acts of inadequacy or negligence committed by an insurer's sales representative (agent or broker) may be covered under **errors and omissions** (E&O), which is a form of liability insurance that protects from such loss occurrence.

The regulation of insurance is done on a state-by-state basis as oppose to the federal level, unlike the banking and securities industry. Federal laws that pertain to insurance include:

> - **Fair Credit Reporting Act of 1971** protects the privacy rights of consumers.
> - **McCarran-Ferguson Act of 1945** establishes state regulation of the business of insurance.
> - **Gramm-Leach-Bliley Financial Modernization Act of 1999** repeals *Glass-Steagall Act* and establishes minimum requirements for state insurance regulations to avoid federal preemption.
> - **Dodd-Frank Wall Street Reform and Consumer Protection Act of 2010** repeals *Gramm-Leach-Bliley Act* and establishes the **Consumer Financial Protection Bureau** (CFPB).

The National Association of Insurance Commissioners (NAIC) is an organization of the 50 state insurance commissioners, and commissioners from the District of Columbia, American Samoa, Guam, Northern Mariana Islands, Puerto Rico, and U.S. Virgin Islands. The purpose of NAIC is to protect the public interest concerning insurance and insurance practices by agents, brokers and insurers, promote a competitive marketplace for insurance, facilitate the fair and equitable treatment of consumers purchasing insurance, promote financial solvency and support the state regulation of insurance. NAIC provides no federal regulatory oversight of the insurance industry.

State regulation of the business of insurance was created by the Court's ruling in *Paul v. Virginia*, which set the business of insurance outside Article 1, Section 8 of the U.S. Constitution ("Commerce Clause"). State insurance commissioners who as members of NAIC subscribe to **model regulations or acts** put forth by the organization for consideration and passage by a state's legislature.

The **doctrine of comity** and **comity of states** are legal principles that hold that one state has deference for the laws passed by another state. In the case of insurance where multiple states may be involved in determining controlling jurisdiction, the laws of the state where the insurer is domiciled will typically be the controlling law for the handling of a first party or third party claim.

A **Buyers Guide to Insurance** is a document that is generally required to be given to an insurance consumer at the time of a sales solicitation. The Buyer's/Consumer's Guide provides the consumer with basic and general information concerning insurance, as well as contact information for help and assistance from the state's insurance commission. The two most common guides for property and casualty insurance are *A Consumer's/Buyer's Guide to Auto/Car Insurance* and *A Consumer's/Buyer's Guide to Homeowners Insurance*.

The **state insurance guaranty association** (SIGA) provides policyholders and beneficiaries with protection against an insurer's insolvency or inability to pay claims. Each state (including Puerto Rico and the District of Columbia) requires membership of all insurers doing business in the state to become a member of the SIGA. Assessments are made of members when insolvency arises, based on the premiums paid by the respective member. Agents, brokers or insurers may not mention the existence of the SIGA to insurance consumers as a matter of law.

Key Definitions

TERM	DEFINITION
Buyer's Guide	Provides insurance consumers with general information about insurance as well as information on who to contact at a state's insurance commission.
Comity of States	See Doctrine of Comity.
Consumer Financial Protection Bureau (CFPB)	An agency established by the Dodd-Frank Act that protects the interests of consumers dealing with financial services (banks, securities and insurance companies).
Doctrine of Comity	The deference of one state's laws to the laws of another.
Dodd-Frank Act	An Act of Congress that repealed Gramm-Leach-Bliley; provides for consumer protection in the financial markets (including banking, securities and insurance).
Fair Credit Reporting Act	Provides privacy protection for consumers.
Gramm-Leach-Bliley Act	An Act of Congress that permitted insurers to engage in investment and commercial banking activities (repealed Glass-Steagall Act). The law also established minimum requirements for state insurance laws in order to avoid federal preemption.
Inadequacy	Obtaining incorrect or improper coverage for the insured.
McCarran-Ferguson Act	An Act of Congress that support state regulation of the business of insurance.
Model Act	Proposed legislation created by NAIC member insurance commissions for states to consider in the regulation of the business of insurance.
National Association of Insurance Commissioners (NAIC)	A membership organization of state insurance commissions for the purpose of protecting the public interest, promoting competitiveness, facilitating the fair and equitable treatment of consumers, promote solvency and support the state insurance

TERM	DEFINITION
	regulatory system.

Chapter Questions

1.   The NAIC is empowered to act in what capacity on behalf of the insurance industry?
A.   Provide support for state insurance regulations
B.   Act as regulatory oversight authority
C.   Protect the interests of consumers
D.   A and C only

2.   The prohibition on insurance companies engaging in the investment banking business is found in what federal act?
A.   McCarran-Ferguson
B.   Glass-Steagall
C.   Dodd-Frank
D.   Gramm-Leach-Bliley

3.   An employee of a company headquartered in Michigan who is located in Ohio would bring a claim of loss against the insured under the laws of which state?
A.   Michigan
B.   Ohio
C.   Both A and B
D.   Either A or B

4.   Information provided to an insurance consumer during solicitation regarding their rights may be referred to as:
A.   Consumer's guide
B.   Buyer's guide
C.   Application
D.   A and B only

5.   What happens to a first party or third party during a claim if the second party goes insolvent?
A.   The claim will not be honored
B.   The claim will be handled by SIGA
C.   The claim will be handled by a bankruptcy court
D.   The claim will be handled by the state's insurance commission

Answer Key

1.   The correct answer is **D**. The National Association of Insurance Commissioners (NAIC) engages in the practice of protecting the public interest; promoting competitive markets; facilitating the fair and equitable treatment of insurance consumers; promoting the reliability, solvency and financial solidity of insurance institutions; and, supporting and improving state's regulation of insurance.

2.   The correct answer is **B**. The Glass-Steagall Act of 1933 (also known as the Banking Act) placed prohibitions on banks, securities and insurance companies from engaging in both investment and commercial banking activities simultaneously.

3.   The correct answer is **A**. Under the doctrine of comity / comity of states principle, the laws of the state where the insured would take precedence and be recognized by the laws of the state in which the claimant is located.

4.   The correct answer is **D**. A consumer's or buyer's guide is provided to consumers during the sales solicitation, providing general and contact information.

5.   The correct answer is **B**. When an insurer (second party) becomes insolvent or fails to meet its claim paying obligation, the claim of a first party (insured) or third party (claimant) goes to the state insurance guaranty association.

GLOSSARY OF TERMS

PRACTICE TEST

1. All of the following are considered unfair claim settlement practices, EXCEPT:

    A) Knowingly misrepresenting relevant facts or policy provisions related to coverage

    B) Offering a direct or indirect inducement for the purchase of policy

    C) Making claims payments without indicating which coverage the payment represents

    D) Attempting to settle a claim for an amount less than what the claimant is entitled

2. Farm liability insurance provides coverage for:

    A) Commercial property owned by the farmer

    B) Personal and commercial vehicles owned by the farmer

    C) Personal assets owned by the farmer

    D) All of the above

3. The name for two policies that are written with identical terms is called:

    A) Primary

    B) Concurrent

    C) Excess

    D) Non-concurrent

4. Which of the following is not one of the five elements of negligence?

    A) Legal duty

    B) Physical harm

    C) Intervening circumstances

    D) Proximate cause

5. What is Coverage D?

    A) Loss of use

    B) Loss of personal property

    C) Loss to other structure

    D) Damage to other structure

6. Under a crime policy, which of the following is not included in the definition for money?

    A) Cash

    B) Money orders

    C) Register checks

    D) Travelers checks

7. A commercial package policy would include all of the following coverages, EXCEPT:

    A) Commercial Auto Insurance

    B) Inland Marine Insurance

    C) Ocean Marine Insurance

    D) Equipment Breakdown Insurance

8. What amount is paid under extra expense coverage?

    A) Expenses that are in addition to normal business expenses prior to a loss

    B) Expenses required for the continuation of the business after a loss

    C) Expenses that are in in addition to normal business expenses after a loss

    D) Expenses required for the continuation of the business prior to a loss

9. In order to be considered insurable, a loss must contain each of the following element EXCEPT:

    A) Definite

    B) Accidental

    C) Catastrophic

    D) Financial

10. What type of damage causes to covered equipment would not be covered under equipment breakdown protection?

    A) Damage caused by electrical failure

    B) Leakage or water damage occurring at a connection point, valve or seal

    C) Equipment parts failure caused by hazardous material or a contaminant

    D) Mechanical failure to a covered piece of equipment resulting in malfunction

11. Which of the following examples is an example of pure risks?

    A) John bets on the NCAA tournament

    B) John fears that a fall on the ice will prevent him from watching the NCAA tournament

    C) A and B

    D) Neither A or B

12. A company that chooses to not produce a product for fear of a potential recall is practicing what method of risk management?

A) Sharing

B) Avoidance

C) Retention

D) Transfer

13. When a party gives up a known right, this is known in legal terms as:

A) Fraud

B) Waiver

C) Misrepresentation

D) Warranty

14. The practice of offering a portion of an agent's commission as an inducement to purchase a policy is known as:

A) Fraud

B) Twisting

C) Rebating

D) Misrepresentation

15. If a vehicle owner's car is damaged by an animal (i.e. deer, bear, etc.), what coverage will pay for the loss under her personal auto insurance?

A) Medical payments

B) Property damage liability

C) Collision

D) Comprehensive

16. Under the provisions of a garage liability policy, which of the following events (loss) would be covered?

A) Damage or injury related to a trailer of the insured maintained in storage in the garage

B) Property damage related to the transportation of the trailer to another garage

C) Damage by vehicles used in organized racing contests

D) Injury resulting from a leased vehicle use by the insured

17. In a homeowner's insurance policy, Coverage C special limit for jewelry pertains to what cause of loss?

    A) Theft

    B) Damage due to fire

    C) Misplaced in a move

    D) A and B only

18. An individual who is a renter would purchase what type of homeowner's insurance coverage?

    A) Homeowners form 1

    B) Homeowners form 2

    C) Homeowners form 3

    D) Homeowners form 4

19. What type of coverage form would NOT provide coverage theft as a loss?

    A) Basic

    B) Broad

    C) Special

    D) All of the above

20. Which of the following is NOT an example of a physical hazard?

    A) A driver ignoring a posted speed limit

    B) A painter improperly positions a ladder

    C) A banana peel is tossed on the floor in a crowded room

    D) An open bottle of rubbing alcohol is left near a baby's crib

21. Which situation best describes the effect of concealment?

    A) Facts deemed material to the issuance of the policy if withheld may result in recession or cancellation

    B) Facts deemed material to the issuance of the policy will result in recession cancellation regardless of whether withheld or not

    C) An insurer may be obligated to reissue the coverage upon discovery of the concealment

    D) A and C only

22. What is the name for an insurer that is owned by its policy holders?

A) Stock

B) Mutual

C) Fraternal benefit society

D) Reciprocal

23. Losses believed to be catastrophic in nature are considered:

I.   Insurable risk

II. Uninsurable risk

III. Ideal risk

A) I only

B) I and II

C) II only

D) I, II and III

24. An unequal exchange between results in a large potential benefit in exchange for a small premium cost is known as what?

A) Cohesion

B) Aleatory

C) Adhesion

D) Comity

25. The commercial property insurance form that provides coverage for a loss caused by fire is:

A) Basic

B) Broad

C) Special

D) All of the above

26. What type of damages are awarded to a party for the actual loss incurred?

A) Compensatory

B) Special

C) Punitive

D) Property

27. What type of liability exists for the owner of a dog when the dog bites a person?

A) Strict

B) General

C) Intentional

D) Absolute

28. Which of the following is NOT a coverage extension available for building and business personal property coverage?

A) Property of others

B) Debris removal

C) Valuable papers and records

D) Non-owned detached trailers

29. A burglary would be covered under a crime policy under what conditions?

A) Forced entry

B) Threat of violence

C) Injury

D) Theft of property

30. Under a BOP, what type of property is NOT covered?

A) Buildings

B) Money

C) Fixtures

D) Furniture

31. Inland marine insurance provides coverage for which of the following?

A) Property in transit

B) Property in transit

C) Property in transit

D) Property in transit

32. All of the following is considered a product under a commercial general liability policy EXCEPT:

A) Finished goods

B) Real property

C) General merchandise

D) A and B only

33. Which of the following types of hazards is described as the blatant disregard for the law or codified standard?

   A) Morale

   B) Legal

   C) Moral

   D) Physical

34. What is not covered under a Farm coverage part?

   A) Crops

   B) Livestock

   C) Farming operations

   D) Farm tractor

35. The sum insured is the amount paid by the insurance company for what?

   A) Partial loss

   B) Total loss

   C) Percentage loss

   D) A and C only

36. The term *"Res ipsa loquitor"* refers to:

   A) What happened speaks for itself

   B) Let the buyer beware

   C) Something for something

   D) The act of the individual is responsible for the result

37. If the policy states that losses to be paid within 30 days upon proof of loss, this refers to which mandatory uniform provision?

   A) Proof of loss

   B) Reinstatement

   C) Notice of claim

   D) Loss payment

38. Employee theft is covered under which type of bond?

A) Fiduciary

B) Fidelity

C) Judicial

D) Surety

39. An insurance organization run by an "attorney-in-fact" is known as:

A) Reciprocal insurance company

B) Mutual insurance company

C) Stock insurance company

D) Fraternal benefit society

40. An insurer's recovery of a portion of the loss paid for an insured's damaged vehicle under a comprehensive auto policy can be accomplished by:

A) Cancelling the policy prior to claim payment

B) Exercising a waiver to its right to assignment

C) Exercising a right of salvage to sell the damaged vehicle

D) B and C only

41. What cost basis is used for calculating physical damage in collision coverage?

A) Full replacement cost

B) Fair market value

C) Actual cash value

D) Agreed upon or stated value

42. Professional liability insurance is:

A) Is the same as errors and omissions coverage

B) Protects the insured from potential loss arising from offering non-professional service

C) Pays fines and penalties associated with a professional claim

D) A and C are correct

43. The law of large numbers is defined as being:

A) The risk of loss is disproportionately spread among a smaller sample

B) Risk must be distributed among a large heterogeneous group of like units

C) Risk must be distributed among a large homogenous group of unlike units

D) Insurance should only be provided to groups with the greatest probability for loss

44. The section of the insurance policy that sets forth rules, duties and obligations of both the insured and the insurance company is known as what?

A) Conditions

B) Declarations

C) Exclusions

D) Benefits

45. The special causes of loss form sets special limits on the amount payable for the loss of certain items. How much is the special limit for letters of credit, stamps, tickets and lottery tickets being held for sale?

A) $100

B) $250

C) $1,000

D) $2,500

46. Supplementary Payments found in liability policies pay for all of the following EXCEPT:

A) Cost of damages in excess of the policy limit

B) Costs and expenses associated with the resolution of claims

C) Reasonable travel expenses

D) Bail bonds

47. The types of risks covered by property and casualty insurance are:

I.   Speculative

II. Pure

III. Real

A) I only

B) II only

C) I and II only

D) I, II and III

48. An insured homeowner that owns a personal auto and homeowner's insurance policy has a car accident resulting in total damage to a covered appliance being transported from a repair store. The damaged appliance loss would be covered by:

A) Personal auto insurance

B) Homeowner's insurance

C) Both A and B

D) Neither A or B

49. An owner of a condominium building would purchase what type of homeowner's insurance coverage?

A) Homeowners form 1

B) Homeowners form 3

C) Homeowners form 4

D) Homeowners form 6

50. In a homeowner's insurance policy design, what percentage of replacement cost would be paid if 75% of the replacement value is insured?

A) 25%

B) 50%

C) 75%

D) 100%

51. What percentage of other structures in a dwelling insurance policy is covered?

A) 0%

B) 10%

C) 50%

D) 100%

52. Policies that allow for open perils provides what type of coverage?

A) Any type of perils

B) Perils not excluded by the coverage

C) Perils that are stated by the coverage

D) A and B only

53. Which of the following lines of authority can be sold by a licensed property and casualty broker or agent?

    I. Liability
    II. Property
    III. Auto
    IV. Disability

    A) II and IV

    B) I and III

    C) I, II and III

    D) I, II, III and IV

54. A pure risk is one that is:

    A) The chance for loss or gain

    B) The chance for gain only

    C) The chance for loss, no gain

    D) The chance for unlimited loss and limited gain

55. Pure risks contain all of the following elements, EXCEPT:

    A) No chance of occurring

    B) Accidental by nature

    C) Can be calculated financially

    D) Spread among a large risk pool of independent units

56. What is an insurer's short rate cancellation?

    A) Earned premium held by the insurer plus incurred expenses

    B) Earned premium held by the insurer less incurred expenses

    C) Earned premium held by the insured plus incurred expenses

    D) Unearned premium returned by the insurer less commissions

57. What cause of loss is not covered in a special cause of loss form for a commercial property insurance policy?

    A) Windstorm

    B) Weight of ice and snow

    C) Specifically excluded perils

    D) A and B

58. The requirement to notify the insurer when a loss has occurred is known as:

A) Notice of claim

B) Time payment of claim

C) Proof of loss

D) Notice of loss

59. Which of the following would NOT be considered part of a commercial package policy?

A) Umbrella

B) General

C) Equipment breakdown

D) Inland marine

60. All of the following are liability exposures that pose a risk for loss to a business EXCEPT:

A) Products

B) Completed operations

C) Premises

D) Theft

61. All of the following are coverage forms for a commercial crime insurance policy EXCEPT:

I.   Loss sustained
II. Discovery

A) I only

B) II only

C) I and II

D) None of the above

62. Which of the following is covered vehicle in a commercial auto policy for loss from physical damage?

A) Automobile

B) Pickup

C) Trailer

D) All of the above is covered

63. Which of the following is NOT considered a dwelling in a dwelling insurance policy?

A) Farm and farm buildings

B) Mobile homes

C) Multi-family residential building

D) A and B only

64. The legal concept that prevents an insurer from the denial of a fact that was previously admitted to be true is known as:

A) Fraud

B) Estoppel

C) Parol Evidence Rule

D) Waiver

65. Which of the following pricing rates modifies class rates lower for positive risk factors and higher for those risk factors that are negative?

A) Scheduled

B) Judgment

C) Merit

D) Individual

66. The payment of the replacement cost for a partial property loss requires what percentage of the home's market value to be insured?

A) 10 percent

B) 50 percent

C) 80 percent

D) 100 percent

67. Which policy provision allows for the interests of each insured, up to the coverage limits, to be treated individually?

A) Indemnity

B) Good faith

C) Severability

D) Liability

68. What type of auto coverage pays for loss due to a vehicle being overturned or crashing into another vehicle?

   A) Collision

   B) Comprehensive

   C) Partial

   D) Total coverage

69. Which of the following coverage protects a business for a non-owned vehicle in its care, custody and/or control?

   A) Drive other car coverage

   B) Personal auto

   C) Commercial auto

   D) Garage keeper coverage

70. Each of the following are elements of a contract EXCEPT:

   A) Legal intent

   B) Legal purpose

   C) Consideration

   D) Authorization

71. Errors & omissions insurance forms provide coverage for:

   A) Defense costs

   B) Auto Accidents caused by employees

   C) Fines levied by an examining authority

   D) Financial penalties

72. The breakdown of equipment covered under the equipment breakdown protection form leads to the breakdown of several (2) additional pieces of equipment which were also covered. Based on the policy form, the total number of breakdowns that occurred are:

   A) 0

   B) 1

   C) 2

   D) 3

73. Which of the following insurance coverage protects an employer from loss arising from claims by its employees?

A) Workers' compensation

B) Employment practices liability

C) Commercial general liability

D) All of the above

74. A company that decides to cancel their commercial auto policy and set aside a reserve to cover any claims arising from accidents involving business vehicles is practicing what method risk management?

A) Control

B) Retention

C) Sharing

D) Avoidance

75. The event or peril that is determined to be most likely the contributing factor for a loss is known as:

A) Intervening cause

B) Proximate cause

C) Strict liability

D) Loss exposure

76. How is the loss ratio for an insurer calculated?

A) Premiums collected divided by combined expenses

B) Earned premiums divided by incurred losses

C) Total expenses divided by total premiums

D) Incurred losses divided by earned premiums

77. Repeated exposure to perils that result in injury or damage that were unexpected and unintended is known as what?

A) Accident

B) Occurrence

C) Condition

D) Risk peril

78. Which of the following is an element of an insurable risk?

    I.   Definite

    II.   Catastrophic

    III. Heterogeneous

    IV. Economic

A) I only

B) II and III only

C) I and IV only

D) I, II, III, IV

79. A local ordinance or code would cause a gap in an individual's homeowner's insurance in which of the below situations?

A) Fire damage loss creating an additional cost because of current zoning laws

B) Requirement for fencing around a swimming pool

C) Local leash law enforced when insured's dog bites someone off the leash

D) A and C only

80. An owner of a single family home would purchase what type of homeowner's insurance coverage?

A) Homeowners form 1

B) Homeowners form 3

C) Homeowners form 4

D) Homeowners form 6

81. Under a property and/or casualty insurance contract, what amount of an insured's insurable interest is recovered after a loss has occurred?

A) 50%

B) 75%

C) 100%

D) 125%

82. The dwelling insurance policy form that provides the broadest coverage is:

A) DP-1

B) DP-2

C) DP-3

D) B and C only

83. Reference to an insurer's protection from insolvency by an agent is:

A) Permitted by law

B) Required by law

C) A violation of law

D) Permissible with proof of coverage

84. What financial obligation does an insurer have under a reinsurance agreement?

A) No financial obligation

B) An amount equal to the retention level

C) The percentage of ceded risk given to risk pool

D) 100 percent of the risk amount

85. Which of the following is an Unfair Claims Settlement practice by an insurer?

I.   Paying an amount that is less than reasonable for a claim by an insured

II. Requiring proof of loss before making payment on a submitted claim

III. Cancelling coverage or reducing benefits due to non-payment of premiums

A) I only

B) I and III

C) II and III

D) II only

86. An agent who is captive is said to be:

A) Surplus lines broker

B) Works for a mutual insurer

C) Represents one line of authority

D) Represents one insurer

87. Each of the following are types of authority given to an agent, EXCEPT:

A) Implied

B) Apparent

C) Granted

D) Express

88. Liability insurance is also referred to as:

A) Errors & omissions

B) Third-party insurance

C) Indemnity insurance

D) All of the above

89. The requirement to pay claims based on the notice of loss is known as:

A) Time payment of claims

B) Notice of loss

C) Proof of loss

D) None of the above

90. Under building and business personal property coverage, which of the following is NOT covered?

A) Supplies

B) Personal property used for business purposes

C) Machinery

D) Land

91. Under Workers' compensation insurance, what type of loss is covered?

A) Injuries at home

B) Sickness, illness or injuries at work

C) Injuries away from work

D) A and B only

92. Which of the following are types of coverages available in a commercial crime insurance policy?

A) Forgery

B) Libel

C) Computer Fraud

D) A and C only

93. A deductible is considered to be what type of risk management technique?

A) Risk sharing

B) Risk retention

C) Risk transfer

D) Risk control

94. Which form provides broad coverage under a dwelling insurance policy?

    A) DP-1

    B) DP-2

    C) DP-3

    D) All of the above

95. What loss exposure is covered through Farm coverage?

    A) Commercial

    B) Personal

    C) Professional

    D) A and B only

96. The part of an issued insurance policy that provides the policy owner with basic policy information is known as:

    A) Definitions Page

    B) Declaration Page

    C) Insuring Clause

    D) Outline of Coverage

97. How many elements are required to establish a case for negligence?

    A) 2

    B) 3

    C) 4

    D) 5

98. Which of the following perils may be excluded in a property coverage form?

    A) Flood

    B) Falling debris

    C) Wind

    D) Fire

99. Which of the following types of coverage provides for strict liability according to the strict liability doctrine?

A) Railroad insurance

B) Owner/contractor protection

C) Builder's risk policy

D) Commercial automobile insurance

100. Coverage that provides protection for the movement of goods on land is referred to as?

A) Ocean marine insurance

B) Cargo insurance

C) Inland marine insurance

D) Trucker's insurance

101. A claim for a Building and Personal property policy must be paid upon receipt of proof of loss by the insurer within how many days?

A) 10 days

B) 15 days

C) 30 days

D) 45 days

102. Under a commercial general liability insurance policy, what medical payments would be covered?

A) Employee

B) Customer

C) Employer

D) Contest participant

103. Under the equipment breakdown protection form, how would an authorization for makeshift repairs be treated for the purpose of helping a business continue production?

A) Expediting expense

B) Errors or omissions

C) Additional expense

D) A and C

104. Who are the parties to a surety bond?

I. Principal
II. Obligee
III. Surety

A) I and III

B) II and III

C) I, II and III

D) III only

105. A potential homeowner purchases a home from an existing homeowner by taking out a loan for a portion of the purchase price from a bank and putting up the remainder amount out of her personal funds. Which of the following parties has an insurable interest in the home?

I. Potential homeowner
II. Current homeowner
III. Bank

A) I only

B) II and III

C) I, II and III

D) I and III

106. Under the National Flood Insurance Program, which of the following is NOT covered?

A) Currency

B) Curtains

C) Plumbing

D) Debris removal

107. Which provision of a homeowner's policy is used regarding a dispute arising between the insurer and the insured over the value of the settlement?

A) Appraisal

B) Right of recession

C) Free look

D) Settlement option

108. Under the provisions of a homeowner's policy, medical payments are made for a loss experienced by:

A) Individual employed by the insured

B) Insured

C) Insured's spouse

D) Leasehold tenant

109. Accidents resulting in loss that occurs under a commercial auto insurance policy are covered in each of the following areas, EXCEPT:

A) United States

B) Puerto Rico

C) Mexico

D) Canada

110. A standard HO-3 form would covered which of the following?

A) A covered auto stolen from homeowner's garage

B) Furniture damaged while being removed from the home during a fire

C) Insured's boat damaged while being towed by the insured's personal auto

D) All of the above

111. An owner of a manufactured home would purchase what type of homeowner's insurance coverage?

A) Homeowners form 1

B) Homeowners form 3

C) Homeowners form 4

D) None of the above

112. The purchase of a dwelling policy should be considered for all of the following reasons, EXCEPT:

A) Insured is looking to supplement their homeowner's insurance

B) The purchaser is not looking for personal liability coverage

C) A person who may not otherwise qualify for homeowner's insurance

D) Am looking for an open peril coverage form

113. A covered item was purchased for $20,000, five years ago and has depreciated by $5,000 today. The replacement cost for the item, which was destroyed in a fire, is $30,000. What is the actual cash value for the item damaged by the fire?

A) $15,000

B) $20,000

C) $25,000

D) $30,000

114. Which of the following represents an ethical activity for a property and casualty agent?

I. Acting in the interest of the insurer
II. Acting in the interest of the agent
III. Acting in the interest of the insured
IV. Acting in the interest of the beneficiaries

A) I and II

B) II and IV

C) III and IV

D) III only

115. Restoring an insured to their original financial value prior to a loss is known as:

A) Indemnification

B) Reciprocal agreement

C) Adverse risk

D) Law of large numbers

116. An agent that engaged in the practice of convincing an insured to lapse their existing coverage in exchange for purchasing a new policy is guilty of what Unfair Trade Practice?

A) Misrepresentation

B) Concealment

C) Rebating

D) Twisting

117. What is the concept of insurance?

A) Risk prevention

B) Risk transfer

C) Risk retention

D) Risk control

118. Which of the following homeowner's insurance form provides the most comprehensive coverage?

A) HO-1

B) HO-2

C) HO-3

D) HO-5

119. Liability insurance provides coverage for what types of acts?

I. Intentional tort
II. Unintentional tort

A) I only

B) II only

C) Both I and II

D) Neither I and II

120. An act of negligence is also referred to as:

A) Tort

B) Criminal act

C) Morale hazard

D) Peril

121. What are the amounts of coverage available for newly constructed building and business personal property that suffers a loss due to damage?

A) $100,000 / $100,000

B) $250,000 / $250,000

C) $250,000 / $100,000

D) $100,000 / $250,000

122. A state that requires employers to provide Workers' compensation benefits for its employees is referred to as:

A) Mandated

B) Elective

C) Compulsory

D) Monopolistic

123. A businessowners policy contains what type of coverages?

   A) Property

   B) Auto

   C) Casualty

   D) A and C only

124. What type of business would purchase a garage coverage form?

   A) Parking lot

   B) Auto dealership

   C) Auto repair shop

   D) Auto repair shop

125. What coverage type under a dwelling insurance policy provides for additional living expenses for a covered loss?

   A) Coverage A

   B) Coverage C

   C) Coverage D

   D) Coverage E

Answer Key

1. The correct answer is B. According to the NAIC's Unfair Claim Settlement Act all of the choices listed are considered unfair acts by an insurer, except for rebating, which is an unfair trade practice listed in the NAIC's Unfair Trade Practices Act.

2. The correct answer is D. Farm liability insurance protects the personal and commercial property owned by the farmer from loss exposure due to a farmer's liability.

3. The correct answer is B. Concurrent describes a two policies issued at the same time with identical terms.

4. The correct answer is C. Intervening circumstances is not one of the five elements needed to establish negligence.

5. The correct answer is A. In a homeowners' policy, Coverage D covers loss of use of the home.

6. The correct answer is A. The word "cash" is not used in the definition for money in a crime insurance policy. "Currency," "bank notes in current use and with a face value," and "coins" are defined as forms of money.

7. The correct answer is C. A commercial package policy, a package of liability and property coverage for businesses, would include each of the listed insurance coverages except for Ocean Marine Insurance.

8. The correct answer is C. Remember, any insurance pays for risk of financial loss created by some peril. That would eliminate choices A and D. Extra expense coverage deals with additional expenses of a business necessary to continue operations after a loss.

9. The correct answer is C. A loss, to be considered insurable must be definite, accidental in nature, produce a financial or measurable economic impact and be spread among a homogenous group of unrelated units. Catastrophic losses are unpredictable in terms of their size and scope and therefore are not considered an insurable risk.

10. The correct answer is B. Damage caused by water or leaks in a covered piece of equipment are excluded in an equipment breakdown protection coverage form.

11. The correct answer is B. Betting is considered a speculative loss, where John has the possibility of both loss and gain. If John were to fall on the ice and be insured as a result, that would be a pure risk resulting in loss only and no gain.

12. The correct answer is B. The company's decision not to manufacture a product for fear of a recall is an example of risk avoidance.

13. The correct answer is B. A party that abandons or gives up a right voluntarily is exercising a waiver of that known right.

14. The correct answer is C. Offering an inducement to an individual as a means to sell insurance is known as rebating, which is an Unfair Trade Practice.

15. The correct answer is D. Loss due to contact with an animal that results in damage to a car under a personal auto insurance policy will be covered under the comprehensive coverage (also referred to as other than collision).

16. The correct answer is A. A garage liability policy provides a benefit for loss related to damage or injury related to stored vehicles covered under the policy, as long as the vehicle remain in the garage. Leased vehicles would be covered under a separate policy provided by the dealer and organized racing cars are not covered.

17. The correct answer is A. Coverage C for certain personal property provides a special limit of up to $1,000 for jewelry due to theft.

18. The correct answer is D. HO-4 provides coverage for a tenant for direct damages resulting in loss.

19. The correct answer is A. The basic coverage form is the least comprehensive of all of the coverage forms available.

20. The correct answer is A. A physical hazard is defined as a condition in the environment that intensifies the probability of a loss. Choices B, C, and D are examples of physical hazards. Choice A would be an example of a morale hazard.

21. The correct answer is A. Concealment, which involved the withholding of facts deemed material to the issuance of an insurance policy, may result in the policy being rescinded or cancelled, once the concealment has been discovered. There is no obligation for the insurer to reissue a policy that has been rescinded or cancelled as a result of concealment.

22. The correct answer is B. A mutual insurer is one that is owned by its policy holders. Stock companies are owned stock holders with shares in the company; a fraternal benefit society is a nonprofit organization that sells policies to members of a society, order or mutual lodge; reciprocal insurers are unincorporated exchanges whose members pay an assessment in the form of a premium to meet expected claims. These exchanges are managed by an attorney-in-fact.

23. The correct answer is C. Losses considered catastrophic are generally uninsurable, with the exception being flood risk.

24. The correct answer is B. An aleatory contract is one where an event (risk, peril) creates the potential for loss, prompting an unequal exchange of value between

the insured and the insurer (premium versus potential benefit.).

25. The correct answer is D. Basic, broad and special cause of loss forms to a commercial property insurance policy cover causes of loss due to fire.

26. The correct answer is A. Compensatory damages are awarded for the actual value of loss incurred by an injured party. Special damages are a form of compensatory damages that are awarded for damages that are tangible (measurable).

27. The correct answer is D. Absolute liability applies to a situation where the owner of a dog is deemed negligent (although not necessarily proven negligent) because of the act of its property.

28. The correct answer is B. Choices A, C and D are all coverage extensions available to building and business personal property coverage. Choice B is additional coverage available at no extra cost for the insured.

29. The correct answer is A. A burglary requires a sign of forced entry (and/or exit) in order to be covered under a crime insurance policy. Threat of violence, bodily injury and theft of property are not necessary elements of the crime of burglary.

30. The correct answer is B. Buildings, fixtures and office furniture are all types of property covered in a businessowners

policy. Money is excluded as property covered in a BOP.

31. The correct answer is D. All of the property listed would be covered by an inland marine insurance policy.

32. The correct answer is B. Real property is not defined as a product under a commercial general liability policy.

33. The correct answer is A. Morale hazard is defined as indifference or disregard to loss because of insurance protection. This may including driving too fast or driving under the influence of drugs or alcohol.

34. The correct answer is A. Choice B, C, and D are covered under a farm coverage part. Crops would not be covered.

35. The correct answer is B. The sum insured is the maximum amount payable by an insurance policy. Based on the choices provided, it would be paid in the case of a total loss.

36. The correct answer is A. The term Res ipsa loquitur refers to a situation where the act speaks for itself. It is often used in cases used to determine liability in the absence of evidence to the otherwise. The Latin for choice B is caveat emptor, choice C is quid pro quo, and choice D is a variation of actus reus or mens rea.

37. The correct answer is D. The loss payment is the uniform mandatory provision that describes the insurer's obligation to pay

claims upon receipt of proof of loss from the insured.

38. The correct answer is B. A fidelity bond is the type of bond issued to protect and employer from acts of theft committed by its employees.

39. The correct answer is A. A reciprocal insurance company is a risk sharing group made up of subscribers and managed by an individual known as an "attorney-in-fact." Each subscriber to the group pays a premium that represents their pro-rata share of risk; if premiums are insufficient to meet claims, an additional assessment is made of the subscribers.

40. The correct answer is C. An insurer may seek to recover some of the loss associated with an insured's damaged vehicle by exercising a right of salvage in order to sell the car. Note that Choice A would be considered an Unfair Claims Settlement Practice.

41. The correct answer is C. Collision coverage provides payments for loss from physical damage caused to a car as a result of colliding with another car or being overturned on an actual cash value of loss. This cost basis prevents an insured from engaging in fraudulent activity in order to receive a benefit potentially greater than the value of the loss.

42. The correct answer is A. Professional liability insurance is also referred to as errors and omissions coverage and provides for the cost of legal defense, judgments and legal settlements connected with the rendering of professional services.

43. The correct answer is C. The law of large numbers states that in order for the risk of loss to be statistically valid it must be distributed amongst a large group of units with unlike characteristics.

44. The correct answer is A. The conditions section of the insurance agreement sets forth all of the terms, rules and obligations of the parties to the contract.

45. The correct answer is B. The special limits set in the special causes of loss forms for lottery tickets held for sale, tickets, stamps and letters of credit is $250. For items such as furs, jewelry, patterns, molds and dies, the amount is $2,500.

46. The correct answer is A. A policy will pay costs up to the stated policy value.

47. The correct answer is B. Insurance (of all types) provides for loss relative to pure risks or those risks that result in loss only and no gain.

48. The correct answer is B. The covered appliance would be listed on the homeowner's insurance policy and covered as personal property.

49. The correct answer is D. HO-6 provides coverage for an insured who is the owner of a condominium or has an ownership interest in a cooperative building.

50. The correct answer is C. If a homeowner's insurance policy covers less than 80% of replacement value, a percentage of the loss will be paid. In this example, if the replacement value were $100,000 and the amount of coverage was $60,000, the amount of coverage would be 75% of the amount required ($80,000). If the loss were calculated at $20,000, $15,000 would be paid and the homeowner would come out of pocket for the difference ($5,000).

51. The correct answer is B. 10% is the limit of insurance coverage for loss to another structure in a dwelling insurance policy.

52. The correct answer is B. An open perils definition in policy coverage provide coverage for perils that are not specifically excluded.

53. The correct answer is C. A property and casualty broker/agent is licensed to sell liability, property and auto insurance, as well as homeowner, commercial, crime, fire, flood and dwelling insurance.

54. The correct answer is C. A pure risk, which is insurable, is described as a chance for loss only, no gain.

55. The correct answer is A. Pure risks are those that are definite, create a financial loss, can be calculated in economic terms, accidental and occur across a large number of unlike (homogenous) units.

56. The correct answer is A. The short rate cancellation of an insurer is calculated as the premiums earned and held plus all of the expenses incurred by the insurer. It is used as a penalty and disincentive to an insured for cancelling a policy prior to the expiration period.

57. The correct answer is C. The special cause of loss form covers loss due to direct physical risk except for those with a special exclusion. It is known as an open perils coverage.

58. The correct answer is D. Notice of loss is the requirement of the insured, typically in writing, that a loss has occurred.

59. The correct answer is A. Commercial umbrella coverage is not part of a commercial package policy, which consists of buildings and business personal property, equipment breakdown, inland marine, crime, general liability, personal (and advertising) injury and business auto.

60. The correct answer is D. Theft is considered an act of dishonesty that would be covered under a fidelity bond.

61. The correct answer is C. Loss sustained and discovery are the types of forms available in a commercial crime insurance policy.

62. The correct answer is A. An automobile is considered a covered vehicle subject to benefits due to loss under a commercial auto policy.

63. The correct answer is A. Farm and farm buildings are excluded from coverage under a dwelling policy; they would be covered under a farm insurance policy.

64. The correct answer is B. Estoppel prevents the denial of a fact if that fact was previously accepted as being true.

65. The correct answer is C. A policy pricing method that bases lower class rates on positive risk factors and higher class rates on negative risk factors is known as a merit rate.

66. The correct answer is C. In a homeowner's policy the replacement cost on a partial property loss (not total) would be payable only if at least 80% of the home's market value is insured.

67. The correct answer is C. The severability of interests clause permits the issuer, subject to the coverage limits, to treat each insured as separate policy owners.

68. The correct answer is A. This question describes collision auto coverage.

69. The correct answer is D. An owner/operator of a parking facility (as an example) would maintain Garage Keepers Insurance as a form of protection against liability arising from loss due to damage (other than collission) to a non-owned vehicle.

70. The correct answer is D. The five elements of a contract include offer, consideration, acceptance, legal intent and legal purpose.

71. The correct answer is A. Coverage provided under an errors & omissions (E&O) insurance policy include costs associated with defending a legal action, judgments and settlements negotiated between parties. Auto accidents, fines and penalties would not be covered in an E&O policy.

72. The correct answer is B. An initial breakdown under the equipment breakdown protection that is the direct cause of additional breakdowns will all be treated as a single loss.

73. The correct answer is B. Employer practices liability coverage provides protection for the employer in the event any claim arises by current or former employees.

74. The correct answer is B. By cancelling their commercial auto insurance coverage and setting aside a reserve for potential future claims, the company is practicing risk retention.

75. The correct answer is B. Proximate cause is defined as the peril with the most significant impact on the resulting loss, particularly when a set of independent factors operate at the same time relative to that loss.

76. The correct answer is D. The insurer's loss ratio is calculated by taking the incurred

loss of the insurer and dividing it by premiums earned.

77. The correct answer is B. An occurrence is a condition that creates the possibility for injury or damage, provided that such occurrence is coincidental and accidental in nature.

78. The correct answer is C. Ideally risks that are insurable occur over a large number of independent and dissimilar units, it is definite, creates financial loss, unexpected, accidental by nature, and measurable in terms of economics. Catastrophic loss is not generally an acceptable risk insurance (with a limited exception for flood insurance).

79. The correct answer is A. Coverage gaps can be created from time to time as local building codes, ordinances and zoning laws are updated. This results in the amount of coverage being inadequate to the actual amount of loss because of the change in law. Of the choices listed, Choice A represents an example of coverage gap for a homeowner's insurance policy.

80. The correct answer is B. HO-3 provides broad based coverage for owner-occupied dwellings, such as a single family home.

81. The correct answer is C. An insured is able to recover up to 100% of their insurable interest upon the occurrence of a loss. A higher amount would represent over-insurance, which may be indicative of fraud or other illegal activity.

82. The correct answer is C. The dwelling insurance form that offers the broadest coverage is the special form, DP-3.

83. The correct answer is C. Reference to a state's guaranty association is not a permissible activity for an insurance agent.

84. The correct answer is B. Under a reinsurance agreement, the amount of financial obligation that an insurer has is equal to their agreed upon retention level.

85. The correct answer is A. Paying an amount on settlement that is less than reasonable for a claim is considered an Unfair Claims Settlement Practice. Requiring proof of loss and cancelling a policy or reducing benefits (during the grace period) for non-payment of premiums are deemed acceptable practices by an insurer.

86. The correct answer is D. An agent that is captive represents the interests of one insurance company.

87. The correct answer is C. Authority given to an agent through the contract is expressed (stated, written); the agent has authority that is implied when dealing with the public in behalf of the insurer; apparent authority is created when an agent exceeds expressed and implied authority.

88. The correct answer is B. Liability insurance is also referred to as third-party

insurance, providing coverage for the first-party (insured) by the second-party (insurer) for the loss suffered by a third-party (claimant). Errors & omissions insurance is a form of liability insurance protection.

89. The correct answer is D. There is no requirement for the insurer to make a payment on a claim without receipt of proof of loss.

90. The correct answer is D. All of the choices listed are covered in building and business personal property coverage except land.

91. The correct answer is B. Workers' compensation pays for loss related to sickness, illness and injuries that are work related (occur on-the-job).

92. The correct answer is D. Acts of forgery and computer fraud are two examples of the coverages available in commercial crime insurance coverage forms.

93. The correct answer is B. Choosing a deductible is considered a form of risk retention.

94. The correct answer B. The dwelling coverage form DP-2 provides broad coverage for losses defined in the basic form (DP-1) plus damages caused by a burglar, weight of ice and snow, loss from damage caused by falling objects, freezing and the discharge of water or steam, which was accidental.

95. The correct answer is D. Farmers' coverage provides loss protection for a farmer's personal and business liability exposure as the loss exposure for a farmer's personal and business property. Professional liability, often called Errors & Omissions (E&O) insurance, provides coverage to those individuals engaged in professional advice services, such as attorneys and medical practitioners (and insurance agents).

96. The correct answer is B. The declaration or "dec" page of the policy provides all of the basic information for the policy owner.

97. The correct answer is D. Five elements need to be present in order to establish a prima facie case of negligence, which are: (1) a legal duty to exercise reasonable care; (2) the failure to exercise such care; (3) physical harm caused by negligent conduct; (4) physical harm as determined by actual damages incurred; and, (5) a proximate cause that harm is within the scope of liability for the negligent conduct.

98. The correct answer is B. A peril, which is the event or action that leads to loss, may be specifically excluded, as in the case of homeowners' coverage. Choices A, C and D are types of perils that may be covered under certain property coverage forms; falling debris is a peril that may be avoidable and subject to a peril exclusion.

99. The correct answer is A. Railroad insurance is a form of coverage that provides benefits related to loss that are

covered by acts of omissions, regardless of fault, in accordance with the doctrine of strict liability.

100. The correct answer is C. Insurance that protects the movement of goods over land is referred to as inland marine insurance.

101. The correct answer is C. An insurer is obligated to pay claims made under a policy upon receipt of proof of loss within 30 days.

102. The correct answer is B. Commercial general liability provide payments for loss due to bodily injury experienced by a customer requiring medical treatment.

103. The correct answer is A. The payment of costs associated with makeshift repairs necessary to help a business resume production while permanent repairs are made to a piece of equipment would be an expediting expense.

104. The correct answer is C. A Surety bond has three parties: the surety, or guarantor who guarantees the performance of the; principal, the second party to; the obligee, the third party.

105. The correct answer is D. Insurable interest is based on the party(s) whose economic interest is impacted the most by a financial loss. In this scenario, the potential homeowner and the bank have an insurable interest in the home.

106. The correct answer is A. Flood policies provide coverage for all of the items listed except currency, precious metals, and other valuables (i.e. stocks and bonds).

107. The correct answer is A. If a dispute between the insurer and insured arises over the value of a settlement in a homeowner's policy, each party will be required to obtain an appraiser.

108. The correct answer is A. The medical payments coverage in a homeowner's policy provides a benefit for injury suffered by an individual employed by the homeowner (i.e. maintenance technician, lawn care specialist, etc.), unless the individual is covered under Workers Compensation. The benefits under the medical payments coverage will not pay for the injury suffered in the home by the insured, spouse of the insured or a leasehold tenant.

109. The correct answer is C. Coverage for accident related loss under a commercial auto insurance policy issued in the United States extends to the U.S., U.S. territories (such as Puerto Rico, Guam, U.S. Virgin Islands, etc.) and Canada.

110. The correct answer is B. The HO-3 basic homeowner's insurance policy form provides broad based coverage for homeowners, including personal property on and away from the home. The homeowner's auto insurance policy would cover theft and damage related to covered vehicles.

111. The correct answer is D. Homeowner's insurance is not available to owners of manufactured or mobile homes; the owner of a manufactured home would need to purchase a special type of insurance coverage specific for mobile homes.

112. The correct answer is A. Dwelling insurance is an alternative (not the same) as homeowner's insurance available to tenants and others who may not otherwise qualify for homeowner's insurance. Dwelling insurance does not provide coverage for personal liability or medical payments resulting from a loss. There are three forms for Dwelling insurance, DP-1 (basic), DP-2 (broad) and DP-3 (special), which covers open perils.

113. The correct answer is C. To determine the actual cash value, the formula would be: Actual cash value = Replacement cost – Depreciation

114. The correct answer is D. Only Choice D represents an agent acting in an ethical manner.

115. The correct answer is A. Indemnification is the process of restoring an insured to their original value after a loss has occurred.

116. The correct answer is D. Twisting is the unfair trade practice of tricking or misleading an insured to lapse existing coverage in favor of purchasing new coverage with the agent.

117. The correct answer is B. The concept of insurance is the transfer of risk from the insured to the insurance company.

118. The correct answer is C. Homeowner's coverage form 3 (HO-3) provides the most comprehensive level of coverage including personal liability and medical payments.

119. The correct answer is B. Liability insurance provides coverage for those acts that are unintentional, also known as acts of negligence.

120. The correct answer is A. An act of negligence is referred to legally as an unintentional tort.

121. The correct answer is C. Under building and business personal property coverage, there is a limit of $250,000 for a newly constructed building and $100,000 for business personal property that experiences a loss due to damage.

122. The correct answer is C. A state with compulsory workers' compensation laws require employers to provide benefits for their employees.

123. The correct answer is A. A businessowners policy (BOP) combines property and liability coverages on a competitive basis for a business than purchasing separate property and liability insurance policies or commercial package.

124. The correct answer is D. A business that parks, repairs or provides storage facilities for a vehicle would purchase garage coverage form for their loss exposure.

125. The correct answer is D. Coverage D provides a benefit for additional living expenses (at a limit of 20% the Coverage A capital amount) for a covered loss.

Exclusive Trivium Test Prep Test Tips and Study Strategies

Here at Trivium Test Prep, we strive to offer you the exemplary test tools that help you pass your exam the first time. This book includes an overview of important concepts, example questions throughout the text, and practice test questions. But we know that learning how to successfully take a test can be just as important as learning the content being tested. In addition to excelling on the Property and Casualty Exam we want to give you the solutions you need to be successful every time you take a test. Our study strategies, preparation pointers, and test tips will help you succeed as you take the Property and Casualty Exam and any test in the future!

Study Strategies

1. Spread out your studying. By taking the time to study a little bit every day, you strengthen your understanding of the testing material, so it's easier to recall that information on the day of the test. Our study guides make this easy by breaking up the concepts into sections with example practice questions, so you can test your knowledge as you read.

2. Create a study calendar. The sections of our book make it easy to review and practice with example questions on a schedule. Decide to read a specific number of pages or complete a number of practice questions every day. Breaking up all of the information in this way can make studying less overwhelming and more manageable.

3. Set measurable goals and motivational rewards. Follow your study calendar and reward yourself for completing reading, example questions, and practice problems and tests. You could take yourself out after a productive week of studying or watch a favorite show after reading a chapter. Treating yourself to rewards is a great way to stay motivated.

4. Use your current knowledge to understand new, unfamiliar concepts. When you learn something new, think about how it relates to something you know really well. Making connections between new ideas and your existing understanding can simplify the learning process and make the new information easier to remember.

5. Make learning interesting! If one aspect of a topic is interesting to you, it can make an entire concept easier to remember. Stay engaged and think about how concepts covered on the exam can affect the things you're interested in. The sidebars throughout the text offer additional information that could make ideas easier to recall.

6. Find a study environment that works for you. For some people, absolute silence in a library results in the most effective study session, while others need the background noise of a coffee shop to fuel productive studying. There are many websites that generate white noise and recreate the sounds of different environments for studying. Figure out what distracts you and what engages you and plan accordingly.

7. Take practice tests in an environment that reflects the exam setting. While it's important to be as comfortable as possible when you study, practicing taking the test exactly as you'll take it on test day will make you more prepared for the actual exam. If your test starts on a Saturday morning, take your practice test on a Saturday morning. If you have access, try to find an empty classroom that has desks like the desks at testing center. The more closely you can mimic the testing center, the more prepared you'll feel on test day.

8. Study hard for the test in the days before the exam, but take it easy the night before and do something relaxing rather than studying and cramming. This will help decrease anxiety, allow you to get a better night's sleep, and be more mentally fresh during the big exam. Watch a light-hearted movie, read a favorite book, or take a walk, for example.

Preparation Pointers

1. Preparation is key! Don't wait until the day of your exam to gather your pencils, calculator, identification materials, or admission tickets. Check the requirements of the exam as soon as possible. Some tests require materials that may take more time to obtain, such as a passport-style photo, so be sure that you have plenty of time to collect everything. The night before the exam, lay out everything you'll need, so it's all ready to go on test day! We recommend at least two forms of ID, your admission ticket or confirmation, pencils, a high protein, compact snack, bottled water, and any necessary medications. Some testing centers will require you to put all of your supplies in a clear plastic bag. If you're prepared, you will be less stressed the morning of, and less likely to forget anything important.

2. If you're taking a pencil-and-paper exam, test your erasers on paper. Some erasers leave big, dark stains on paper instead of rubbing out pencil marks. Make sure your erasers work for you and the pencils you plan to use.

3. Make sure you give yourself your usual amount of sleep, preferably at least 7 – 8 hours. You may find you need even more sleep. Pay attention to how much you sleep in the days before the exam, and how many hours it takes for you to feel refreshed. This will allow you to be as sharp as possible during the test and make fewer simple mistakes.

4. Make sure to make transportation arrangements ahead of time, and have a backup plan in case your ride falls through. You don't want to be stressing about how you're going to get to the testing center the morning of the exam.

5. Many testing locations keep their air conditioners on high. You want to remember to bring a sweater or jacket in case the test center is too cold, as you never know how hot or cold the testing location could be. Remember, while you can always adjust for heat by removing layers, if you're cold, you're cold.

Test Tips

1. Go with your gut when choosing an answer. Statistically, the answer that comes to mind first is often the right one. This is assuming you studied the material, of course, which we hope you have done if you've read through one of our books!

2. For true or false questions: if you genuinely don't know the answer, mark it true. In most tests, there are typically more true answers than false answers.

3. For multiple-choice questions, read ALL the answer choices before marking an answer, even if you think you know the answer when you come across it. You may find your original "right" answer isn't necessarily the best option.

4. Look for key words: in multiple choice exams, particularly those that require you to read through a text, the questions typically contain key words. These key words can help the test taker choose the correct answer or confuse you if you don't recognize them. Common keywords are: *most*, *during*, *after*, *initially*, and *first*. Be sure you identify them before you read the available answers. Identifying the key words makes a huge difference in your chances of passing the test.

5. Narrow answers down by using the process of elimination: after you understand the question, read each answer. If you don't know the answer right away, use the process of elimination to narrow down the answer choices. It is easy to identify at least one answer that isn't correct. Continue to narrow down the choices before choosing the answer you believe best fits the question. By following this process, you increase your chances of selecting the correct answer.

6. Don't worry if others finish before or after you. Go at your own pace, and focus on the test in front of you.

7. Relax. With our help, we know you'll be ready to conquer the Property and Casualty Exam. You've studied and worked hard!

Keep in mind that every individual takes tests differently, so strategies that might work for you may not work for someone else. You know yourself best and are the best person to determine which of these tips and strategies will benefit your studying and test taking. Best of luck as you study, test, and work toward your future!

Made in the USA
Las Vegas, NV
18 June 2022